Cambridge Ele

Elements in Global C
edited by
Ching Kwan Lee
University of California-Los Angeles

GLOBAL CIVIL SOCIETY AND CHINA

Anthony J. Spires
The University of Melbourne

CAMBRIDGE
UNIVERSITY PRESS

Shaftesbury Road, Cambridge CB2 8EA, United Kingdom

One Liberty Plaza, 20th Floor, New York, NY 10006, USA

477 Williamstown Road, Port Melbourne, VIC 3207, Australia

314–321, 3rd Floor, Plot 3, Splendor Forum, Jasola District Centre, New Delhi – 110025, India

103 Penang Road, #05–06/07, Visioncrest Commercial, Singapore 238467

Cambridge University Press is part of Cambridge University Press & Assessment, a department of the University of Cambridge.

We share the University's mission to contribute to society through the pursuit of education, learning and research at the highest international levels of excellence.

www.cambridge.org
Information on this title: www.cambridge.org/9781009507523

DOI: 10.1017/9781009183925

When citing this work, please include a reference to the DOI 10.1017/9781009183925

First published 2024

A catalogue record for this publication is available from the British Library.

ISBN 978-1-009-50752-3 Hardback
ISBN 978-1-009-18416-8 Paperback
ISSN 2632-7341 (online)
ISSN 2632-7333 (print)

Global Civil Society and China

Elements in Global China

DOI: 10.1017/9781009183925
First published online: April 2024

Anthony J. Spires
The University of Melbourne
Author for correspondence: Anthony J. Spires, anthony.spires@unimelb.edu.au

Abstract: This Element traces the history of and recent developments in the unstable relationship between global civil society (GCS) and China. It analyzes the normative impacts GCS has had on China – including the Chinese state and domestic civil society – and the possibilities created by Beijing's new "going out" policies for Chinese civil society groups. It examines the rhetoric and reality of GCS as an emancipatory project and argues that "universal values" underpinned by principles of human rights and democracy have gained currency in China despite official resistance from the government. It argues that while the Chinese party-state is keen to benefit from GCS engagement, Beijing is also determined to minimize any impact outside groups might have on regime security. The Element concludes with some observations about future research directions and the internationalization of Chinese civil society.

Keywords: global civil society, China, NGOs, democracy, universal values

ISBNs: 9781009507523 (HB), 9781009184168 (PB), 9781009183925 (OC)
ISSNs: 2632-7341 (online), 2632-7333 (print)

Contents

1 Global Civil Society as a Normative and Political Project

China's relationship with global civil society (GCS) has evolved in fits and starts over the past several decades and remains unstable today. This is understandable, given that the international nongovernmental organizations (INGOs) that comprise GCS have long touted universal values of human rights and democratic participation as core to their missions. This Element traces the development of this unstable relationship, starting around the turn of the twenty-first century and moving to the present. I make the overall argument that while the past few decades have shown China is keen to benefit from GCS engagement – and that "universal values" have gained currency in China – Beijing is determined to minimize any impact outside groups might have on the Chinese Communist Party (CCP) and the security of its regime. I also analyze the impacts GCS has had on China and the possibilities created by Beijing's new "going out" policies for Chinese civil society groups.

The normative principles that have become ubiquitous in the vision and mission statements of established GCS actors over the past few decades were perhaps inevitably going to invite conflict with the political preferences of Beijing. Yet this was not always so clear. Deng Xiaoping's opening to the outside world in the 1980s and the fall of the Soviet Union led many optimists to believe that major political reform was on Beijing's agenda. In a sign of openness, in the 1980s China invited some INGOs and international organizations to share their expertise on issues like higher educational reform, disaster relief, and poverty alleviation. But the brutal suppression of the Tiananmen Movement of 1989 put an almost immediate freeze on further exchanges, and doubts soon arose as to whether Deng's economic reforms could proceed and whether political change was off the table. Then, in 1992, Deng's "southern tour" reaffirmed the commitment to economic opening. Around the same time, Beijing successfully convinced the United Nations to grant China hosting rights for the Fourth UN World Conference on Women in 1995. Parallel to that gathering, an NGO forum brought women's rights groups from around the world to Beijing, where Hillary Clinton famously declared that "human rights are women's rights, and women's rights are human rights."

Beijing's tolerance of these events in the mid 1990s hinted that the party-state might be willing to bestow some political legitimacy on women's rights and on China's nascent civil society. As more INGOs entered the country, the topics they were allowed to work on expanded to include issues like environmental protection and children's rights. In the late 1990s, the US-based Carter Center was even invited to help monitor village-level elections, an almost unthinkable development just two decades earlier. Yet from the vantage point of late 2023, the future of GCS in China does not look so bright. Over the last decade, Beijing has overseen a crackdown on domestic civil society, promulgated a comprehensive INGO Law requiring registration with the national police, and taken a host of other actions that collectively reveal the fragility of GCS engagement in China. Enjoying increasing wealth and confidence, Beijing is also no longer a passive player in the international realm. The party-state has taken a series of steps to "go out" into the world, setting the stage for Chinese government-organized NGOs (GONGOs) and even grassroots civil society organizations to pursue humanitarian, developmental, and environmental projects overseas.

   To illustrate the changes in the relationship between GCS and China, and the possibilities that lie ahead, I draw on the broader literature on global civil society and that on China itself. Although my own research on this topic began in late 2004, much of the perspective I present here is informed by data I collected between early 2014 and early 2017 as part of an investigation into the survival strategies of INGOs in China. Over this period, I conducted seventy-two semi-structured interviews with sixty-eight INGO representatives, foreign and Chinese government officials, foreign donors, grassroots Chinese NGOs, and Chinese academics. I also organized two focus groups with INGO leaders in Hong Kong, all of whom had extensive program activity in mainland China. In addition, I conducted participant observation and an online survey concerning the initial draft of China's 2017 INGO Law. Research efforts on changes after the INGO Law's implementation continued sporadically into early 2023 with follow-up interviews with some previous research contacts as well as a small number of new activists and organizations in China and abroad. These research efforts have greatly informed my own understandings of the field and shaped what I have chosen to highlight in this Element.

GCS: Origins and Applications of a Concept

To begin making sense of China's engagement with global civil society, we must recognize that it is a contested concept. Depending on the analyst, it is a term that conveys the hope of the Enlightenment or a phenomenon that threatens to undermine national sovereignty and diminish democratic accountability. Probably no one has done more to explicate the meanings of GCS and propagate it as an idea than Helmut Anheier, Marlies Glasius, and Mary Kaldor through their early work as editors of the annual volume, "Global Civil Society." They see GCS as "a sphere of ideas, values, institutions, organizations, networks, and individuals located between the family, the state, and the market, and operating beyond the confines of national societies, polities, and economies" (Anheier, Glasius and Kaldor 2001, p. 17). Yet their understanding of the concept also has a strongly normative and political dimension, emphasizing the emancipatory potential of interconnected groups of progressive people around the world and arguing that civil society (global and otherwise) is "about managing difference and accommodating diversity and conflict through public debate, non-violent struggle, and advocacy" (Kaldor, Anheier and Glasius 2005, p. 2).

If GCS is a "sphere," international NGOs are the most recognized organizational instantiation of the ideas and values that animate it. In the first Global Civil Society yearbook, its editors argue that the growth in numbers of and connections between INGOs in the 1990s gave form to what we call GCS today:

> The number of organizations and individuals that are part of global civil society has probably never been bigger, and the range and type of fields in which they operate never been wider: from UN conferences about social welfare or the environment to conflict situations in Kosovo, from globalized resistance to the Mutual Agreement on Investments to local human rights activism in Mexico, Burma, or Timor, and from media corporations spanning the globe to indigenous people's campaigns over the Internet. (Anheier, Glasius and Kaldor 2001, p. 4)

Emerging as part of a post-Cold War vision of an increasingly democratic world, the concept according to John Keane implies "the contemporary thickening and stretching of networks of socio-economic institutions across borders to all four corners of the earth, such that the peaceful or 'civil' effects of these non-governmental networks are felt everywhere." In tangible form, it is comprised of "organizations, business initiatives, coalitions, social movements, linguistic communities and cultural identities" that share "at least one thing in common: across vast geographic distances and despite barriers of time, they deliberately organize themselves and conduct their cross-border social activities, business, and politics outside the boundaries of governmental structures, with a minimum of violence and a maximum of respect for the principle of civilized power-sharing among different ways of life" (Keane 2001, p. 24).

Normative projections feature heavily in other scholars' analyses as well. In her own separate treatment of the subject, Mary Kaldor (Kaldor 2003) suggests that global civil society could serve as an antidote to the state of war that engulfs whole regions of the world at any given point in time, positing that GCS provides "a way to supplement traditional democracy . . . it offers the possibility for the voices of the victims of globalization to be heard if not the votes." Reflecting the reasoning of nongovernmental organizations (NGOs), like the Red Cross, who claimed they deserved a seat at the table when the structure of the United Nations was being developed following WWII, Kaldor argues that GCS promotes a democratic inclusivity by creating "new fora for deliberation on the complex issues of the contemporary world, in which the various parties to the discussion do not only represent state interest" (Kaldor 2003, p. 148). Activist scholars Korten, Perlas, and Shiva (2002) depict GCS as "a popular resistance movement challenging the institutions and policies of corporate globalization" (Korten, Perlas and Shiva 2002, n.p.).

Not everyone has been so willing to see rights-based morality and democratic virtue as the defining traits of GCS, however. Anderson and Rieff (2005) take a skeptical view of its utility as a concept, emphasizing the undemocratic context of INGO advocacy – "because, plainly, international society is not democratic" (Anderson and Rieff 2005, p. 30). The people of the globe do not "elect" the leadership of Greenpeace, for example, yet the organization claims to represent the interests of all people on Earth as well as Earth itself. Reflecting conservative fears of supranational authorities, historian John Fonte asserts that "an entire industry of transnational agencies and nongovernmental organizations is pushing forward changes designed either to deny or override the national sovereignty of democratic states" (Fonte 2004, p. 117).

To be sure, while progressive ideals and democratic visions may cross borders easily, global power inequalities – embodied by, among other things, immigration controls to developed countries – ensure that people themselves are not always as physically mobile. If, therefore, "the victims of globalization" are to find their voices and de facto political representation through INGOs, we might expect that they need to be primary constituents of, or at least active participants in, the organizations themselves. For INGOs to be truly representative of this disempowered interest base, that is, we might reasonably expect to find INGOs emanating from, or at least encompassing, the societies or social groups most adversely affected by globalization.

Yet this would be a mistaken view of GCS, even by its proponents' own accounts. Keane depicts the vulnerability and limits of global society in stark terms, writing that "global civil society is currently a string of oases of freedom in a vast desert of localized injustice. ... Inequalities of power, bullying, and fanatical, violent attempts to de-globalize are chronic features of global civil society" (Keane 2001, pp. 38–39). Anheier et al., for their part, find that the locations of Keane's "oases" are biased toward a certain geographical area. In their first GCS yearbook, they note that "in particular, *one of the most striking findings of the Yearbook is that global civil society is heavily concentrated in north-western Europe*" (Anheier et al. 2001, p. 7 [emphasis in original]). Twenty years later, it seems the geography of INGOs still greatly informs the ways in which power is exercised within GCS. In their detailed study of whose voices contributed to developing the Sustainable Development Goals at the United Nations, Sénit and Biermann conclude that "global civil society is largely organized and funded by people in the Global North. There is simply no effective control by Southern actors of those civil society organizations that speak in their name" (Sénit and Biermann 2021, p. 589).

Trenchant critics of INGOs and GCS more broadly have argued that the norms, values, and programs of GCS represent and promote the interests and perspectives of wealthier countries and global capital. An early camp of dissenters, writing around the same time as Anheier et al., see in the normative aspects of GCS a danger equal to or greater than its potential for good. Tvedt argued that "it is possible to interpret foreign and national NGO communities as representing elite interests . . . with the role and impact of basically maintaining the status quo" (Tvedt 1998, p. 209). Political theorist Andre Drainville (2005) argued that GCS is simply the cultural handmaiden to neoliberal capitalist interests, so deeply intertwined with the capitalist world order that we should not expect it to lead to the articulation or promotion of any alternate sort of politics. Similarly, Peck and Tickell (2002) argue that the success of neoliberalism in the 1990s succeeded in shrinking the space for political change in such a way that its fundamental precepts have become "common sense" in the Gramscian use of the term, projecting a "depoliticized" vision of civil society that masks its neoliberal operations. Gaby Ramia (2003) suggests that INGOs have been increasingly under pressure to emulate the "strategic management" practices of the governments and transnational corporations that fund them.

In the roughly twenty years since the GCS concept was articulated by Anheier et al., other scholars have deepened critiques and marshalled empirical evidence to demonstrate how GCS struggles to live up to a normative vision based on rights and freedoms. Whether and how certain issues become recognized as "rights" by GCS actors has itself become an object of study. Scholars like Clifford Bob have led a broader examination of "the development of new international rights and the strategic interactions between aggrieved groups and the human rights movement," asking how grievances on the ground become translated into normative claims that are later adopted by the "gatekeepers" of the INGO world (Bob 2009, p. 4).[1] Charli Carpenter has shown how the predicament of children born of wartime rape have been subsumed under the larger issue of gender-based violence rather than taken up as a problem deserving its own focus (Carpenter 2009), raising further ethical questions about the power of INGO coalitions and networks to promote or suppress recognition of particular rights (Carpenter et al. 2014).

Cooley and Ron's case studies of INGO aid efforts in Bosnia and the Democratic Republic of Congo show "how powerful institutional imperatives

---

[1] The phenomenon of new rights recognition within GCS, as I argue later, has pushed Chinese authorities to adapt to and engage with shifting rights expectations over the past two decades.

can subvert INGO efforts, prolong inappropriate aid projects, or promote destructive competition among well-meaning transnational actors," allowing them to conclude that "attempts by INGOs to reconcile material pressures with normative motivations often produce outcomes dramatically at odds with liberal expectations" (Cooley and Ron 2010, p. 206). In their work and that of others, the distinction between value-driven, progressive nonprofits and profit-driven or management-driven firms rapidly begins to blur. As Lecy, Mitchell, and Schmitz put it in their study of transnational advocacy NGOs, "advocacy organizations are not exclusively principled *or* self-interested," but rather "can be understood as dynamically constrained impact-maximizers" that are internally diverse and should not be painted with one broad brush (Lecy, Mitchell and Peter Schmitz 2010, p. 247). More recently, Schmitz and Mitchell (2022) offer a somewhat more sympathetic response to the criticisms of transnational NGOs (TNGOs, their preferred term). They point out that the vision of TNGOs has expanded tremendously over the past two decades, while the legal and institutional "architecture" that shapes them remains little changed. In their analysis, TNGOs have "transformed from conventional charitable intermediaries seeking to ameliorate deprivations to self-proclaimed agents of fundamental change committed to . . . the solving of major social, political, economic, and environmental problems" (Schmitz and Mitchell 2022, p. 12).

In sum, the rosier image of GCS suggests a system or process by which the woes of rampant capitalism can be addressed and disadvantaged people empowered. Skeptics and critics of GCS, on the other hand, see the global collective of INGOs as a threat to the autonomy of sovereign states, as limited in impact because they themselves are internally undemocratic, or as handmaidens to corporate interests. Rather than a growing number of Keane's "oases" necessarily leading to a better life for the world's most marginalized, studies such as these suggest that GCS often serve to privilege certain people's voices and interests over those of others. Many of these concerns about rights and democracy are also key to understanding GCS vis-à-vis China, and, as I argue later in this Section and in Section 2, the potential (or threat) of GCS as a normative project has certainly captured the imagination of the Chinese party-state. Before moving to a more focused consideration of China, however, first I turn to another perspective on how GCS might support progressive social movements – through "transnational activist networks" (TANs).

Transnational Activist Networks

Emerging almost in historical parallel with the earliest articulations of GCS is the concept of TANs, a term coined by international relations scholars Keck and Sikkink (1998) to refer to "networks of activists, distinguishable largely by the centrality of principled ideas or values in motivating their formation" (Keck and Sikkink 1998, p. 1). In Keck and Sikkink's original book on the topic, they used the TAN concept to analyze global achievements made in the twentieth century in the fields of human rights, environmental protection, and women's rights, but in the last two decades it has been widely applied to a range of movements and solidarity structures, including those involving China. Foreshadowing Beijing's concerns about "hostile foreign forces" attempting to destabilize and delegitimize CCP rule, Keck and Sikkink suggest that TANs are distinctive because:

> by building new links among actors in civil societies, states, and international organizations, they multiply the channels of access to the international system ... [and] make international resources available to new actors in domestic political and social struggles. By thus blurring the boundaries between a state's relations with its own nationals and the recourse both citizens and states have to the international system, advocacy networks are helping to transform the practice of national sovereignty. (Keck and Sikkink 1998, pp. 1–2)

The knowledge-sharing and norm diffusion aspects of how TANs operate have particular relevance to China today, as Keck and Sikkink suggest that:

> at the core of network activity is the production, exchange, and strategic use of information. This ability may seem inconsequential in the face of the economic, political, or military might of other global actors. But by overcoming the deliberate suppression of information that sustains many abuses of power, networks can help reframe international and domestic debates, changing their terms, their sites, and the configuration of participants. When they succeed, advocacy networks are among the most important sources of new ideas, norms, and identities in the international system. At the same time, participation in transnational networks can significantly enhance the political resources available to domestic actors. (Keck and Sikkink 1998, p.x)

Three elements within their explication of TANs can be analyzed independently when looking at China – information exchange, new ideas, and networks. First, as is widely understood today, Beijing works vigorously to control the "the production, exchange, and strategic use of information" through massive online and offline surveillance practices, censorship, and monitoring of communication between domestic and overseas civil society actors. In the twenty-odd years since Keck and Sikkink's book was published, the technologies of control Beijing regularly deploys have increased dramatically in both scope and capability. The Chinese government continuously seeks to insulate its population from what it deems incorrect information and corrupting influences from the outside world. On the second element, however, there is ample evidence to suggest that TANs have served as "important sources of new ideas, norms, and identities" exerting immeasurable impact within China, a topic I take up in depth later, in Section 2.

On the third element, the impact of TANs on China appears limited again, as evidence suggests that "participation in transnational networks" has done little to enhance the political resources of Chinese domestic civil society actors. Rather, networking has often made them targets of state repression simply by virtue of their international connections, a motivation to repression that analytically stands apart from the nature or content of any claims they may make upon the state. Proscriptions against "colluding" with foreign forces, as written into Hong Kong's 2020 National Security Law (NSL), and harming "national security," as written into the PRC's 2017 INGO Law (Sidel 2019), are only two of many recent indications that for domestic activists the simple fact of foreign contact is justification enough for suspicion and repression, independent of the actual substance of an actor's field of work. As far back as 2005, if not earlier, the jailing, harassment, and banning of any number of civil society actors – feminist activists, human rights lawyers, environmental NGOs, and LGBTQ organizations, just to name a few – have been justified in part or in whole by claims that the Chinese people involved are working as agents of nefarious foreign forces. While difficult to distinguish the causal significance of foreign networking in specific instances of repression, its recurring rhetorical use indicates the state's conviction that ties alone constitute a threat that demands action.

The Limited Efficacy of TANs in China

As compelling a vision as TANs offer for making sense of new modes of international solidarity and progress on issues like human rights, environmentalism, and other issues, even Keck and Sikkink themselves, writing from the vantage point of the late 1990s, are explicit in arguing that TANs are unlikely to impact policy change in authoritarian regimes like China. They offer the example of how human rights organizations in the 1990s resorted to urging the "drastic" approach of revoking most-favored-nation status to pressure Beijing, a tactic that worked only until President Bill Clinton moved to de-link trade and human rights when agreeing to China's fifteen-year quest to join the World Trade Organization (WTO) in 2001. With opposition to China's WTO admission persisting in Congress and among human rights activists, the US Congressional Executive Commission on China (CECC) was established as a political concession to China's critics in Washington. Over the past two decades, the CECC's annual reports detailing continuing abuses and restrictions on civil and political rights in China have not stopped the rapid integration of China's economy with that of the USA. Yet "integration" with the USA and the broader global capitalist order does not mean the USA or TANs have particular leverage to produce progress on human rights issues in China.

As Keck and Sikkink wrote even before China's accession to the WTO, "the Chinese case is negative substantiation for the argument presented here: a weak, repressed, and divided domestic movement, combined with little possibility for leverage politics, constitutes exactly the conditions under which we would not expect successful human rights pressures" (Keck and Sikkink 1998, p. 118). Indeed, at the time of their writing, the very notion of an "NGO" was still relatively new in China, having been popularized in the lead-up to the 1995 United Nations Women's Conference and only slowly spreading into other realms of activity (Zhang 2001; Spires, Tao and Chan 2014). In the two decades since China's WTO accession, while Chinese civil society has grown markedly, the Chinese state's countermeasures have proven effective at maintaining a "weak, repressed, and divided domestic movement," a situation that has only intensified since Xi Jinping came to power in 2013. Over the past ten years, from a crackdown on human rights lawyers to labor rights NGOs and feminist activists, the state has methodically reduced space for civil society, with some groups closing up shop, some co-opted by the state, and others forced to find less public ways to pursue their goals (Yuen 2015; Fu 2017; Tian and Chuang 2022).

Making Sense of GCS in China: From TANs to Norm Socialization

Analysts of Chinese civil society broadly agree that TANs and the "boomerang effect" posited by Keck and Sikkink continue to be largely ineffective at effecting change within China. In a study of six major transnational campaigns targeting China, for example, Noakes (2018) found that only in ones where the CCP itself saw some advantage in shoring up its domestic rule did TANs have any apparent impact. Advocates of Tibetan independence, justice for Falun Gong practitioners, the abolition of the death penalty, and caps on carbon emissions found little to no resonance in state policies or actors, leading to a fizzling out of transnational efforts on those fronts (Noakes 2018). While foreign calls to strengthen intellectual property rights law and improve HIV-AIDS programs met with greater success, these were largely, in Noakes' analysis, due to the state's own interests in moving on these issues, not because of outside pressure. Rather, the key to changes in these areas was that Beijing's "policy priorities are set with a keen eye trained on domestic legitimacy and the consequences of a given action (or inaction) for the stability and survival of CCP rule" (Noakes 2018, p. 163).

The field of HIV-AIDS activism in China has been extensively studied as a means to understand dynamics involving the party-state, domestic and foreign NGOs, and intergovernmental organizations. Examining funding for HIV-focused grassroots NGOs, Timothy Hildebrandt found that grassroots groups' explicit appeals to the Global Fund, which was for many years the largest international nongovernmental donor for HIV causes in China, went unheeded. As one grass-roots group was told, "because the Global Fund is 'country-led' and relies on a strong partnership with the governments of those countries in which it operates, it 'will not impose or pressure governments to do one thing or another'" (Hildebrandt 2013, p. 128). Yan Long's work on transnational AIDS organizations shows how international pressure on China yielded not an empowerment of domestic groups, but "the adoption of indirect, covert, and nonviolent operations to both deter and control the domestic AIDS movement" (Long 2018, p. 311). Fengshi Wu's analysis of transnational AIDS activism offers a further critique of the TAN argument, noting that the contentious politics framework underpinning Keck and Sikkink's formulation ignores the complicated realities of how microlevel politics works in the case of China:

> It is as if there were no face-to-face political bargaining, direct communica-tion, and indirect mutual influence between the NGOs and the targeted government. In addition, it underestimates the power of non-confrontational means in politics. Non-confrontational means range from persuasion, social-ization, policy recommendation, project demonstration to public education. They often do not spark headline news and stay low-profile, making them more difficult to detect and research, yet they are proven to be indispensable for establishing new norms, standards and principles. (Wu 2011, p. 626)

While politics in China may not play out in the same ways as it does in democratic states, the CCP does not rule without some give and take vis-à-vis its own population, a phenomenon made all the more apparent by the sudden about-face abandonment of China's COVID-Zero policy in December 2022 following inten-sive protests and months of widespread dissatisfaction with lockdowns and eco-nomic hardship. Despite being an outlier in the international system – as both the most populous country in the world and the world's largest authoritarian state, among other things – the Chinese state has nonetheless been deeply impacted by the rules and norms of the international system since Deng Xiaoping launched his "reform and opening" program in 1979 (Kent 2002; Morton 2005; Wang 2007, 2016; Wu 2011; Bewicke 2016; Lewis 2020). As Wu argues in her overview of the "norm socialization" literature in international relations, "long-term engagement in multilateral and bilateral settings across issue areas, such as security, human rights, women's rights, legal reforms, and environmental protection," has shaped how both the Chinese state and the individual officials understand and approach a wide range of issues (Wu 2011, p. 627).

Indeed, although today it is widely recognized that Deng's bold "opening" to the outside world has had tremendous economic impacts on China in economic terms, the country's increasing integration into the global system over the last four decades has also wrought significant changes in China's domestic political and social life. As Hongying Wang (2007) documents, "linking up with the international track" – an official slogan appearing first around 1987 – was originally intended to help justify economic reforms but quickly became widely used to support any number of policy innovations purported to be "the norm" outside of China, including in the political and social realms. Through the 1990s and into the early 2000s, Wang writes, "a minority of Chinese intellectuals have voiced their vision of China adopting the prevailing international 'social morals.' Their voice is weak now, but it may grow stronger as the larger political atmosphere changes" (Wang 2007, p. 22).

In sum, while TANs may be integral to the Chinese state's reactions and responses to the "threat" of GCS, as an analytical framework it is still limited if we understand the goal of TANs as leading to policy change and directly empowering local civil society actors. Rather, as I argue in Section 2, through a GCS lens we can begin to see how – parallel to state socialization – a wide range of liberal–democratic ideals and concepts have been embraced by Chinese civil society. Arguably, it is this nonstate social realm where global civil society's impact will ultimately prove most meaningful and consequential for China.

2 The Impacts of GCS on China

If, as outlined in Section 1, GCS was originally broadly conceived as a norma-tive project underpinned by universal values of human rights and democracy, how has it managed to have any impact at all on the world's largest authoritarian state? In this section, I take up this question, arguing that decades of engagement and interactions between the Chinese party-state, Chinese civil society, and international NGOs have in fact deeply affected both the Chinese government and domestic civil society actors. To support these claims, I consider a series of questions about both the normative impacts and the practical consequences of GCS engagement in China and trace the key dynamics that have shaped the relationship.[2]

How Structurally Integrated Is China into Global Civil Society?

In contrast to China's reputation as "the workshop of the world" and a central player in the global economy, available data indicate that China is, structurally speaking, likely to be on the furthest periphery of global civil society (GCS).

---

[2] My approach here focuses on the impact GCS has had on China. As Stephen Noakes and Jessica C. Teets have demonstrated, however, the peculiarities and demands of China's authoritarian state have also caused INGOs to adapt the ways they pursue their work inside China (Noakes and Teets, 2020).

This was true at the turn of the twenty-first century when China entered the WTO in 2001, and remains true two decades later, despite China playing an increasingly important global economic role. In 2005, Anheier, Glasius and Kaldor (2005) published an analysis of the INGO membership density of 180 countries. The more memberships held by individuals or organizations in a country, the greater the country's structural embeddedness in GCS. In their figures, based on 2003 data, China's INGO membership density was estimated at only 1.9 members per million persons. China thus ranked lowest in membership density of all 180 countries included in their survey, below the world average of 45.4 memberships per million, below the 37.8 memberships per million average of all middle income countries, and also below the 17.7 memberships per million average of all lower income countries (Anheier, Glasius and Kaldor 2005, pp. 304–309).

In fact, China's membership density in INGOs may have been even lower than it appeared in the Anheier et al. data. Because the INGO figure provided by Anheier et al. includes both China-based individual members and organizational members of INGOs, and because the Chinese government has enjoyed a virtual monopoly on the establishment and creation of formally registered NGOs, any Chinese organizational members of INGOs would most likely be GONGOs, not the grassroots groups outside observers might assume them to be.

Chinese GONGOs have sought to join INGOs for a variety of reasons. As one civil servant working in a government agency explained to me in 2005, his agency's GONGO:

> was created to make it easier to talk with foreigners, because foreigners would usually prefer to deal with NGOs instead of the government. ... This type of organization benefits the [agency] in two ways. First, it allows them to talk with foreigners. Secondly, when they wear their "NGO hat" they can leave China more easily to attend conferences, workshops, etc. In their official capacity it's harder for them to get out of the country.

The same phenomenon still holds today. The PRC's Confucius Institutes – most of which have been shuttered in the USA recently (Yang 2022) – have been a key but controversial part of China's global soft power push since the early 2000s (Zhou and Luk 2016; Theo and Leung 2018; Repnikova 2022). After coming under fire as suspected agents of the Communist Party, Confucius Institutes in some countries have recently re-branded themselves under the aegis of a nonprofit GONGO, the Chinese International Educational Foundation (CIEF). Registered under the Ministry of Civil Affairs in China and founded in 2020, the CIEF says it "is dedicated to supporting projects of Chinese International Education worldwide, promoting people-to-people exchanges, enhancing understanding among countries, and thus contributing to mutual learning and exchanges between the diverse civilizations in the world" (Chinese International Education Foundation 2023). Although it is unclear whether CIEF has joined any education-focused INGOs, it could easily do so and thus be misread as "just another" cultural or charitable group focused on education.

Although the Anheier et al. data are now two decades old and not easily replicable, there is some evidence to suggest that China may actually be *less* structurally integrated into GCS today. China's growing wealth has been a factor in driving international donors to rethink their China engagement. The Global Fund, a major donor to the fights against HIV-AIDS, tuberculosis, and malaria in China starting in 2003, chose to leave China in 2014 after refocusing its efforts on poorer countries. Distributing over US$800 million in grants over a ten-year period and "active in more than two-thirds of China's counties and districts, the Global Fund was the largest international health partner in the country."[3] Its departure highlighted international donors' frustrations with Chinese restrictions on grassroots civil society but did not deter other donors, like the Gates Foundation, which in 2023 announced a grant of US$50 million to Tsinghua University for the development of drugs to fight infectious diseases.[4]

While major donors may disagree on the viability and desirability of working in China, in structural terms China's decreasing direct contact with GCS is perhaps most evident when we consider the steps Beijing has taken since 2003 to restrict INGOs' physical accessibility to the country and to limit the scope and flexibility of their operations inside its borders. Following the Color Revolutions in former Soviet states – including Kyrgyzstan, on China's border – the Chinese government established extra measures to restrict and monitor financial flows from INGOs and other donors (Wilson 2009). Although grassroots groups had been largely sidelined from the bulk of philanthropic monies flowing from US donors to China (Spires 2011b; Kellogg 2012), the specter of the Color Revolutions put Beijing on heightened alert to cooperation between grassroots and foreign organizations.

In the early to mid 2000s, due to political barriers hindering registration as a "proper" NGO, many Chinese grassroots NGOs found that one way to survive as a formal organization was by registering as a for-profit business (Spires, Tao and Chan 2014). As Beijing sought to choke off the flow of foreign funds to groups it deemed a threat, in 2010 the State Administration of Foreign Exchange enacted a new regulation requiring Chinese entities – businesses in

---

[3] https://aidspan.org/?action=catelog_singlepost&id=13166 – Accessed August 30, 2023.

[4] www.forbes.com/sites/russellflannery/2023/06/15/gates-foundation-to-donate-50-million-partner-with-beijing-and-tsinghua-to-fight-infectious-disease/?sh=64d5d1964465 – Accessed August 30, 2023.

particular – to apply at their bank for permission to receive foreign donations, offering information such as a signed agreement between the donor and recipient specifying the funds' uses.[5] This regulation impacted the relatively privileged grassroots groups that had managed to directly receive foreign funds, forcing a rethink of their financial support bases and often heightening their visibility to authorities. In at least one prominent case, that of Beijing-based HIV-AIDS group Aizhixing, suspicion of financial irregularities was the reason given for raiding its office in December 2010 and confiscating documents related to its work and finances.[6] The group's founder, Wan Yanhai, had earlier in the same year gone into self-imposed exile in the USA out of concern for his family's security.

Categorizing and Controlling

The 2010 foreign donation regulations were, in effect, a formalization and legitimization of controls governing the relationship between domestic groups and INGOs that would eventually take fuller form in the 2017 INGO Law. Although trade and industry associations were a large cohort of the INGOs active in China before the INGO Law – and remain so after its promulgation – given the normative aims attributed to GCS my interest here lies not in business-focused groups but rather in foreign nonprofit organizations whose missions are driven by "politically sensitive" concerns like human welfare, education, healthcare, and human rights. While the Chinese state is happy to do business with many overseas entities and for trade associations to help facilitate those relationships, it is this noncommercial category of INGOs that is more likely to risk stepping over the "red line" laid down by the political priorities of the authoritarian state. And, indeed, it is these sorts of organizations that have animated most scholarship and inquiries into GCS in China. As a shorthand, I refer to these groups as "progressive" INGOs, although within China they are typically spoken of – in hushed tones – as "sensitive" (*mingan*) organizations, a label that can be applied to both domestic and foreign civil society groups.

In 2013 – some ten years after Anheier et al.'s data were generated – I undertook a desktop survey of INGOs active in China, utilizing extensive contacts in the field of both domestic and foreign NGOs, government contacts, academic contacts, and publicly available online data. This effort identified just over 200 progressive INGOs working in China at the time. In using the word "foreign," I include in the object of study here – as does China's own INGO Law – the "special administrative

[5] www.safe.gov.cn/en/2009/1230/700.html – Accessed December 30, 2022.
[6] For a summary of their situation in 2010, see www.cecc.gov/publications/commission-analysis/tax-officials-investigate-chinese-ngo-aizhixing-founder-advised-not.

regions" of Macau and Hong Kong, as well as Taiwan. The law avoids the politically constructed "foreign" (*waiguo*) – which would exclude organizations from these three places – by using the term *jingwai*, or "outside the borders [of mainland China]," to denote all the "outside" groups it seeks to regulate. As I explain below, the 200-odd groups I found is a small minority of the 7,000 INGOs the Ministry of Public Security claimed to be operating in China around the same time.

Between 2013, when Xi Jinping took office, and 2017, when the INGO Law took effect, the landscape of INGOs in China changed dramatically, a shift that is even more apparent from the vantage point of 2023. Substantively, what has diminished in the wake of the INGO Law are focused efforts by GCS actors to promote human rights and the rule of law. Of the INGOs with registered offices in China between 2017 and mid 2022, over half were trade and industry associations, and half of the "temporary activities" approvals given to INGOs were focused on education, a government-favored field that poses the least risk to foreign actors.[7] Rule of law promoters like the American Bar Association, once in active partnership with state lawmaking organs as well as grassroots NGOs, have closed down their work in China after failing to achieve legal registration. Asia Catalyst, a group that provided grassroots NGO capacity-building on rights-related topics, has shifted its work to other countries. Other rights-focused groups came into greater conflict with authorities after the law came out or in the lead-up to the law's finalization. The most famous of these was the notorious case of Peter Dahlin, cofounder of the Chinese Urgent Action Working Group. His activities and predicament were well-publicized inside and outside China when in early 2016 he was detained and compelled to give a publicly televised confession of his crimes (organizing an unauthorized NGO), leaving his Chinese colleagues still in detention after he was deported from the country. The messages such actions send are unambiguous to both INGOs and their would-be Chinese staff and other supporters – INGOs with an explicit focus on advocacy and rights-based work are not welcome. People working with these types of groups are, like Dahlin, at personal risk of imprisonment and must carry the burden of all the uncertainty and distress that entails.

To the extent that INGOs employ foreign staff – which even before 2017 was becoming less common – those foreign staff may enjoy a relatively easy exit should they run afoul of authorities, the case of Peter Dahlin notwithstanding. Domestic grassroots groups, by contrast, have no such fallback when encountering the same problems. And although the notion of "overseas" (*jingwai*)

---

[7] www.chinafile.com/ngo/latest/major-questions-about-chinas-foreign-ngo-law-are-now-settled – Accessed December 29, 2022.

NGOs is specified by the law to include Hong Kong-based NGOs – these comprise a large percentage of the progressive INGOs active in China – the NSL for Hong Kong, imposed by Beijing in 2020, means that Hong Kong citizens' involvement with INGOs places them at special risk of being accused of "collusion" with "foreign forces" deemed threatening to China's national interests. The INGO Law also details a number of penalties and punishments for breaching its proscriptions against a range of vaguely worded activities undertaken in the mainland.

Since 2017, at least one foreign group has been publicly chastened by Chinese authorities and forced to close their China operations after running afoul of the law. China's state-run *Global Times* newspaper reported in 2021 that Australia-based Nying-Jey Projects for Tibetan Communities had been issued a warning by the police in Sichuan's Garze Tibetan Autonomous Prefecture for operating without authorization.[8] The group had been working since 2002 to provide financial support for nunneries and educational sponsorships for Tibetan children in China and India. After having its funds confiscated by local Chinese authorities in 2021 and threatened with fines and imprisonment if it continued operations, the group shifted its work entirely to monks and Tibetan-in-exile communities in India.[9] As others have also observed, putting the Ministry of Public Security in charge of the law's enforcement and administration is meant to send a clear signal that the law is both an administrative tool and a legal justification for penalizing unsanctioned activities (Sidel 2019).

As China's INGO Law was being drafted in 2015, GCS actors had begun to take note and worried it would mean the end of their China work. The leader of a Hong Kong-based INGO with an office in Beijing told me at the time: "If this law passes, most INGOs will leave! Everyone will just stop their work in China!" These worries quickly reached the ears of top leaders. At an event hosted in Seattle by the National Committee on US-China Relations, Xi Jinping seemingly sought to reassure GCS actors who were worried about the law's impacts, declaring:

> China recognizes the positive role played by foreign non-profit organizations. So long as their activities are beneficial to the Chinese people, we will not restrict or prohibit their operations, but will protect their operations through legislation and protect their legitimate rights and interests. On their part, foreign NPO's in China need to obey Chinese law and carry out activities in accordance with law. (Xi 2015)

---

[8] www.globaltimes.cn/page/202105/1223453.shtml – Accessed December 29, 2022.
[9] www.njp.org.au/wordpress/wp-content/uploads/2021/07/202106-NJP-newsletter.cleaned.pdf – Accessed December 29, 2022.

Yet despite what was interpreted by some as a sign of goodwill and indication that the law would not unduly restrain GCS work, registration numbers since 2017 show that the INGO Law has indeed become a major barrier to overseas NGOs. Prior to the INGO Law's promulgation, the Ministry of Public Security (which ultimately was given responsibility for INGO registration and legal enforcement) estimated there were 7,000 INGOs active in China. By other officials' accounts with whom I spoke, this was likely an overestimation. Yet in March 2023 – six years after the law took effect – only 686 INGOs had actively registered representative offices.[10] That is, less than 10 percent of the number of groups estimated by the Ministry of Public Security to be operating in China before 2017 had successfully registered under the INGO Law. This is not for lack of trying. In just one example, Greenpeace East Asia, which has a large office and many staff in Beijing, as of late 2023 is still "in the process" of registering – tolerated by authorities, and also carefully surveilled, but not yet allowed to legally and fully register.

In sum, since the early 2000s Beijing has taken calculated and clear steps to reduce the already limited structural ties linking GCS and Chinese domestic groups and to limit the activities of INGOs it deems sensitive or threatening. The message sent to the world (and China's own citizens) is simple – the extent and nature of China's ties to INGOs will be determined by the government of China, not domestic grassroots groups, not other Chinese actors, and certainly not the agents of GCS.

CCP Concerns about INGOs and Foreign Influence

As outlined in Section 1, the broader scholarly debate over the import and impact of GCS *outside* of China involves two main poles of contention. In simplified form, on one side of the debate are the proponents of global civil society who see it as means through which liberal–progressive values, democracy, and human rights are increasingly being embraced across any number of countries and sociocultural contexts. In this view, GCS is truly emancipatory, an outgrowth of the Enlightenment ideals of individual rights and freedom. This view holds that it is through the workings and spread of GCS that humanity can learn to overcome our differences and avoid armed conflict. Skeptics of GCS, however, contend that its emancipatory potential is limited either because it is simply too structurally undeveloped or concentrated in a few particular regions or countries, or – more darkly – that GCS is an extension of a neoliberal economic agenda that promises to liberate while actually working to further

---

[10] https://ngo.mps.gov.cn/ngo/portal/toInfogs.do?p_type=1# – Accessed March 31, 2023.

marginalize the voices of people occupying the lowest echelons of global power.

Both perspectives on the impacts of GCS can find justification in ground-level realities within China. The normative, emancipatory promise of GCS has resonated with many in China and impacted the state as well as domestic civil society. The critique of neoliberalism animating many GCS critics is also meaningful for China, as ideas and practices as diverse as NGO "capacity-building" (Spires 2012) and "venture philanthropy" (Lai and Spires 2021) – both imported from abroad – find common ground in the apolitical, business-oriented version of civil society that they subtly promote. While the broader literature's two main concerns are important ones, they generally assume ease of entry into China and, more fundamentally, tend to obscure or overlook the role of the CCP party-state in setting the rules of the game over not just GCS entry but also its normative and practical impacts.

Given Beijing's fears that INGOs, as agents of GCS, could foment a "color revolution" in China, it is the political dimension of GCS that has captured the attention of the CCP over the past two decades. To be sure, since the 1990s, hundreds of millions of dollars have flowed into the country from INGOs and foreign donors, although the 2017 INGO Law and the COVID-19 pandemic have contributed to a restriction of those flows. Alongside those monies have come INGOs' rhetorical support for grassroots civil society and an emphasis on "universal values" concerned with human rights and democratic accountability. Despite the rhetoric, however – and its perceived threats to the party-state – many Chinese government agencies and GONGOs have actually been the direct beneficiaries of foreign funding, not the grassroots groups that are typically seen as potential threats to social stability and CCP rule (Spires 2011b). For the better part of two decades, these contrasting realities fueled internal debates over whether INGOs are good for China or a danger too great to bear.

During fieldwork in China in early 2005, I heard concerns about foreigners trying to destabilize China through support of domestic civil society organizations, a theme that continuously arose – sometimes directly, sometimes obliquely – in my conversations with academics and government officials. Around that time, Zhao Liqing, a professor at the Research Office for International Strategy of the Central Party School in Beijing, neatly summarized the debate over INGOs in an article widely reprinted in the Chinese press:

> There are currently two opposed views on foreign NGOs in China. One of them demonizes foreign NGOs, the other "angel-izes" them. The demoniza-tion view emphasizes the negative aspects of foreign NGOs, seeing them as coming to China with some ulterior motive in mind, attempting to harm our national security and national interests by promoting a "color revolution."

The positive view of foreign NGOs, on the other hand, affirms the good aspects of their work, seeing them as representatives of the people that promote justice and humanity. In this "angel-ized" view, foreign NGOs have come to China to alleviate poverty, solely helping others with no thought for personal gain. (Zhao 2006)

Zhao noted that there was a great diversity in the types of programs funded by foreigners, but they found willing partners in virtually every corner of Chinese society:

Foreign NGOs running programs in China usually work with Chinese part- ners. The form of cooperation varies greatly, from simply providing funds for a Chinese organization's research, meetings, and operations, to participating in the design of the Chinese partner's programs or implementing some of the foreign NGO's own programs. Foreign NGOs are now finding Chinese partner organizations in every sector of society, including national-level Communist Party organizations, government agencies, the National People's Congress, the National Political Consultative Conference, the Communist Youth League, the All-China Federation of Trade Unions, the Women's Federation, universities, and research institutes. Partners also include nonprofit, private educational and research institutions, GONGOs (government-organized NGOs), and so-called "grassroots organizations." (Zhao 2006)

Reflecting the unresolved debates within the party-state, Zhao noted that the positive aspects of foreign NGO activity in China are multiple, including bringing in funding; bringing in foreign experience, information, personnel, and ways of running activities; helping China's social development; assisting the construction of a new social system in China; helping improve public policy processes in China; and helping construct the rule of law in China. At the same time, however, he also acknowledged possible negative aspects of foreign NGO activity in China, including harming national security, harming the political stabilization of the country, promoting corruption, and pushing foreign models onto China. Zhao ultimately concluded that, on the whole, foreign NGOs help more than they harm, but cautioned that it was difficult to foresee the potential long-term negative consequences of their actions.

Zhao's essay, published in 2006, aimed to provide a more "balanced" view of GCS' impact on China. In the latter years of Hu Jintao's government and especially since Xi Jinping took charge in 2013, however, suspicion toward domestic and foreign civil society actors has only grown sharper. Two accounts in official Chinese publications indicate the shift to an unreservedly strident party line on civil society and "foreign forces." In an influential 2011 article in the state publication *Qiushi*, Zhou Benshun – then the Secretary General of the influential Central Political and Legal Affairs Commission – rejected the very idea of "civil society" (*gongmin shehui*), calling it a "trap" laid by Western forces to bring down the party and overthrow the state (Zhou 2011). In 2013, Wang Shaoguang, a political scientist at the Chinese University of Hong Kong, published an article in an online forum of *The People's Daily* describing "civil society" as inappropriate for China, vague to the point of being useless, and a "crude myth" fabricated by neoliberalism. In its stead, he argued, China should aspire to a "people's society" (*renmin shehui*), as "the people" was already commonly used in terms like "the people's police," "the people's government," and "The People's Bank" (Wang 2013). Another official warning about the dangers of INGOs came in 2013, when China's Minister of Civil Affairs publicly stated that some INGOs may be engaging in illegal activities and that the regulations governing them are insufficient (China Times 2013). During this period, a blanket ban on the term "civil society" was introduced on media organizations throughout the country, and academics in the field learned to studiously avoid using it in publication titles and public lectures.

Most famously, in April 2013, a "Communiqué on the Current State of the Ideological Sphere" – later known as "Document #9" – was issued by the CCP's Central Committee and circulated to all lower-level party organizations around China (ChinaFile 2013).[11] It laid out several ideological challenges China faced, including two directly connected to GCS. The first of these, "Promoting 'universal values' in an attempt to weaken the theoretical foundations of the Party's leadership," argues that proponents of universal values "believe Western freedom, democracy, and human rights are universal and eternal. This is evident in their distortion of the Party's own promotion of democracy, freedom, equality, justice, rule of law, and other such values." The Communiqué goes on to explain that "the goal [of such slogans] is to obscure the essential differences between the West's value system and the value system we advocate, ultimately using the West's value systems to supplant the core values of Socialism." In short, it asserts that while the CCP's own formulation of "core socialist values" (*shehui zhuyi hexin jiazhi*) includes the concepts of freedom, democracy, equality, justice, and rule of law (Gow 2017), these are fundamentally different from those promoted by the agents of GCS. Conflating the two, the Communiqué concludes, can be "confusing and deceptive" to Chinese people. However, the document does not elaborate on what the differences might be. It is noteworthy that despite the widespread acknowledgment that Xi Jinping has consolidated power into his own hands since coming to

---

[11] The following quotations from Document #9 are taken from the ChinaFile translation (ChinaFile, 2013).

power, he has not renounced the Party's rhetorical aspirations to democracy (*minzhu*), using the term forty-nine times in his October 2022 speech to the 20th National Party Congress in Beijing (Xi 2022).

A second "challenge" Document #9 depicts involves foreign forces "promoting civil society in an attempt to dismantle the ruling party's social foundation." Here, civil society is said to have:

> been adopted by Western anti-China forces and used as a political tool. Additionally, some people with ulterior motives within China have begun to promote these ideas. ... Viewing civil society as a magic bullet for advancing social management at the local level, they have launched all kinds of so-called citizen's movements. ... Advocates of civil society want to squeeze the Party out of leadership of the masses at the local level, even setting the Party against the masses, to the point that their advocacy is becoming a serious form of political opposition.

The promotion of civil society – something that many GCS actors in China had been doing publicly for at least a decade before 2013 – was, with this document, officially labelled a serious ideological threat to China and to the CCP. Keenly aware of the increasing scrutiny, in 2014, one INGO offering training and financial support to Chinese legal activists pursuing rights defense work had chosen to mimic the self-limiting strategy of domestic NGOs (Spires 2011a; Hildebrandt 2013): "We're intentionally keeping ourselves at a small scale because of the administrative and management burdens of getting larger, and to avoid attention. ... We don't have much contact with Chinese NGOs. We want to keep it at a minimum. We need our low profile."

The larger political environment outside China also contributed to heightened concerns about GCS. As Franceschini and Negro (2014) argue, it is no coincidence that the sorts of statements and restrictions mentioned here came soon after the Arab Spring, which sparked fears in Beijing about the potential inspiration of a "Jasmine Revolution" in China. Fears of instability instigated by foreign NGOs also intensified in the leadup to Hong Kong's explosive 2014 Occupy Central and Umbrella Movement protests. The leaders of Occupy Central were publicly planning their actions in early 2013, launching a series of public forums and "deliberation days" that attracted many members of the Hong Kong public but also the attention and ire of national security officials in mainland China (Chan 2015). As a semiautonomous "special administrative region" and a former British colony, Hong Kong people had long enjoyed freedom of assembly and speech, and the city's government had for decades allowed an annual and very public commemoration of the 1989 Tiananmen Movement organized by Hong Kong civil society. Historically, Hong Kong had also served as a base for European and American missionaries, charities, and – in more recent decades – a range of GCS actors seeking to operate programs and influence society and politics inside mainland China. All of this was clearly known to authorities in Beijing and, arguably, somewhat tolerated if not fully accepted. Yet with Xi Jinping in office barely a year and seeking to consolidate party control, in early 2014 China's Ministry of State Security implemented a two-month, nationwide investigation meant to ferret out dangerous "overseas" elements inside the Chinese mainland and the organizations they represent. Mainland NGOs with ties to overseas groups – including those based in Hong Kong – were visited by national security officials, required to produce statements detailing all past and current projects involving INGOs, and in some cases had their bank accounts frozen.

Almost ten years on from the Occupy and Umbrella Movements, Hong Kong has a new NSL that also seeks to limit the influence of foreign NGOs. A number of foreign groups (and also many of Hong Kong's homegrown civil society organizations) have closed up shop since the law was imposed by Beijing in 2020, with Amnesty International being perhaps the most famous of these. In announcing their decision to leave the city, the chair of Amnesty's international board wrote that the NSL "has made it effectively impossible for human rights organizations in Hong Kong to work freely and without fear of serious reprisals from the government" (Amnesty International 2021).

More recent academic analyses from scholars in China serve to shore up the political judgments underpinning the 2017 INGO Law and Hong Kong's NSL. Xu Han, of the Wuhan Municipal Party School's Theory Center, wrote in 2020 that the USA was leading the way for other Western countries to use INGOs to threaten the values, culture, and ideology of China in a new "political war" targeting China (Xu 2020). Dai Fengning (2020), at Renmin University's School of International Relations, depicts a continuing effort on the part of the USA to foment color revolutions in Eastern Europe via INGOs, to destabilize Belt and Road Initiative (BRI) projects in countries along China's southwestern borders, and to destabilize Hong Kong with US government-funded NGOs like the National Endowment for Democracy (NED). INGOs, Dai argues, "use the West's discourse power on the international stage, use so-called 'universal values' like democracy, freedom, human rights and environmental protection ... to confuse the masses' thinking, eventually changing their behavior, inciting them to engage in street protests and street rebellions to overthrow the current leaders" (Dai 2020, p. 121). Flipping Zhao Liqing's (2006) cautious but optimistic conclusion on its head, Dai argues that China should be highly vigilant and on guard against the role American NGOs play in US foreign policy.

In sum, since the turn of the twenty-first century, the Chinese state has taken a series of repressive actions toward domestic and GCS actors over fears that they are threats to CCP rule. Developments of the past decade reveal that the earlier internal debate about the role INGOs should play in China has been resolved decidedly in favor of extreme caution. What limited scholarship exists within Chinese academia typically reaffirms state suspicions of overseas entities such as INGOs, private philanthropic foundations, and foreign state-supported organizations, often ignoring questions of whether they are officially sanctioned by legal registration in China or otherwise working in partnership with Chinese government entities. There is little to debate concerning the status of GCS in China at the moment. From the standpoint of Beijing, many foreign NGOs are suspect and most likely working in the service of hostile foreign governments.

The Subtle Yet Intentional Blurring of Distinctions between Foreign State and Nonstate Actors

To comprehend the hardline policy decisions taken by Beijing, understanding broader societal perceptions of charity in China can be instructive. At least to some extent, the perception that foreign NGOs work on behalf of foreign governments is, from the CCP's perspective, reasonable and seemingly "natural." Take just the superficially neutral term "donor" as an example. The term "donor" is used widely now in the broader scholarly literature on development and aid to "developing countries." It is conceptually distinct from the INGOs and domestic NGOs that operate and implement programs on the ground or carry out advocacy work. Within China, foreign sources of funding for Chinese grassroots NGOs – and for the GONGOs and government agencies that have benefited from foreign donor funds in the past – are often lumped together under one category, regardless of whether the donor is technically a private foundation, an INGO that makes grants, or a foreign government agency. On the ground in China, it is often seen simply as "*guowai de qian*" – foreign money.

Within government agencies, and even within Chinese grassroots NGOs, the perception often exists that foreign foundations are likely to be direct tools of their home country governments, or that, even if there is independence in name, in reality they are probably somehow controlled by the home country government. This perception has multiple roots, but there are at least two contributing factors. One is bewilderment about why foreign donors would want to support civil society development in China. Charity for the sake of charity is a notion that meets with a great deal of skepticism even within a totally domestic setting (Farid and Song 2020). Bringing in non-Chinese donations raises even more doubts. And given the increasing centrality of the market economy in China over the past few decades, many people are hard-pressed to believe that foreigners would give money to Chinese causes without expecting something tangible in return.

A second factor contributing to the belief that foreign foundations and governments are cut from the same cloth also stems from the reality of life in China. The close ties between China's official civil society – GONGOs and government-backed foundations – and the Chinese government are well known in China's civil society and of course in the government itself. There is a general perception that GONGOs, paid for and supported by the government, simply do the bidding of the government. Believing that these ties are real and durable in China, many people suspect this must also be true for foundations and governments in the USA and other countries. In the case of money from the USA, for example, there is sometimes a suspicion that American foundations – including the Ford Foundation, which is quite prominent in China's development world – are in league with the US government. "I think they probably have similar goals, right?," one NGO leader I interviewed asked with a knowing half-smile, implying that in the case of the USA, the goal is to work against the Chinese government. In this worldview, money from foreign foundations and money from foreign governments becomes the singular "foreign money," implying a common fund as well as a common political agenda.

Politically, this blurring of domestic government and nongovernment philanthropic donors serves to reinforce the CCP's preferred narrative that the party is the state and that the state is the people. Eliding state and nonstate sources of charity – whether looking abroad or within China – also helps further the CCP's vision of a society that serves state goals, glossing over scholarly and popular distinctions between state and society that party leadership views as anathema to its continued rule. Denying any such distinctions allows the Party to justify its increasingly ambitious control over civil society, its funding to NGOs that fall in line through "purchase of services" agreements (Zhao, Wu and Tao 2016), and its stringent and careful surveillance of funding flows from foreign sources who, in the feared scenarios of a Color Revolution, might look like they are coming to China's aid but could in reality be plotting to undermine China's political status quo.

INGOs: A Sheep in Wolf's Clothing?

Yet, how should we assess the threat to the Chinese party-state from GCS? In structural and simple numerical terms, Beijing has little to be concerned about. As already noted, the data collected by Anheier et al. (2005) show when the Color Revolutions came on to the radar screen for the Chinese government, around 2005, international NGO membership within China was the lowest in their dataset of 180 countries.

Aside from INGO memberships and offices, another avenue through which GCS could be imagined to impact China is through financial flows from overseas philanthropic organizations. Yet, here again, the numbers suggest GCS is more of a sheep in wolf's clothing than a substantial threat to CCP rule. In an earlier study, I analyzed funding flows from US-based private foundations to Chinese grantees between 2002 and 2009 (Spires 2011b). Over this eight-year period – which roughly covers the time of the first "Color Revolution" (arguably, the 2003 Rose Revolution in Georgia) until just after the global spectacle of the 2008 Beijing Olympics – American private philanthropic donors spent almost US$450 million on over 2,500 grants to Chinese recipients. While that figure may seem large – especially if one presumes the grantees are the kinds of disruptive grassroots groups that Beijing has long feared – a more detailed analysis reveals that the vast majority of funds did not go to grassroots NGOs. Rather, GONGOs, academic institutions (which are government-controlled in China), and government agencies received the vast majority of this philanthropic support, accounting for 86 percent of monies sent. Grassroots groups, by contrast, received only about 5.6 percent. Moreover, the majority of funds – almost 70 percent – went to Beijing-based recipients, making for much easier monitoring by the various central government institutions most concerned about foreign influences on Chinese society. I attributed this to a kind of "organizational homophily," a process in which the personal preferences of elite-led US funders and institutional pressures from both China and the USA converge to systematically disadvantage grassroots NGOs (Spires 2011b). A more detailed study of European grantmakers should be undertaken, but as one European foundation representative explained to me in 2014, "working with local NGOs is not a priority because we see them as still very weak. But we always try to bring NGOs to the table at any events. They're always on our radar."

Even if the majority of funding has not gone to grassroots groups, sceptics might question whether Chinese civil society has still been used by hostile "foreign forces" to foment unrest or political instability in China. One way of addressing this question is to look at foreign donor support for civil society development. Many UK-, Hong Kong-, and US-based donors and INGOs – and, to be sure, those from any number of democratic countries active in China – have long expressed publicly a commitment to "building" Chinese civil society. From the standpoint of global development studies, this is not surprising. Since the collapse of the Soviet Union in 1991, academics, INGOs, private philanthropic foundations, and international and supranational institutions like the United Nations and the World Bank have maintained at least a rhetorical focus on civil society as a broad social good that deserves financial and logistical support.

One tangible form of nonmonetary support from GCS to Chinese civil society comes in the form of training programs that purport to help professionalize emerging domestic NGOs. Training programs are a common kind of support offered by INGOs and international donors to local civil society organizations in many parts of the world. In a study of two such "capacity-building programs" designed by GCS actors active in China (Spires 2012), I found that they largely conveyed ideas and practices designed to create professionalized NGOs that were structurally and operationally similar to those in North America and thus more in line with donors' expectations of what grant recipients should look like. These multiday workshops were the two most prominent such programs in China in the mid 2000s and attracted hundreds of "trainees" from a wide range of grassroots NGOs and GONGOs. In terms of content, the two programs – both developed in North America based largely on experiences in the USA and Canada – were similar. Their main themes concerned the role of the board of directors, leadership, accountability, governance, volunteer management, and financial management. Both programs concluded with what many grassroots NGO attendees suggested was arguably the most valuable "lesson" to be taken away – how to fundraise. I characterize these as "donor-driven" training programs because, although purportedly developed in discussion with "Chinese partners," they largely reflected the concerns of US-based donors. At the same time, Chinese grantees – the target clients of these programs – often resisted these agendas, arguing that some imported structures are impractical in China's context or inappropriate for newly emergent Chinese NGOs.

Viewed more broadly, the nonprofit management agendas promoted in for-eign-originated training programs are politically and economically conservative. For funders who want to expand or continue their involvement in China, a rhetorical commitment to democracy and community empowerment, coupled with practical emphasis on professionalization and hierarchical management, is well-aligned with the interests and rhetoric of the Chinese party-state. For Chinese leaders who do not want to lose control over civil society, the lessons flowing into China about NGO management are also not especially threatening. The structures and practices which they promote mesh well with popular business management principles embraced by the state, while also serving to channel potentially unruly social energies into predictable and governable organizational forms.

Further evidence supporting this argument can be found in the ways the Charity Law, promulgated in 2016, dictates the shape and forms legally regis-tered "charitable organizations" (*cishan zuzhi*) should take.[12] Drafting of the law itself began around 2005 with the translation of charitable regulations from some thirty-odd legal jurisdictions around the world. The result – a decade in the

---

[12] An English translation of the law can be found on China Law Translate, at: www.chinalawtran slate.com/en/2016-charity-law/ – Accessed January 7, 2023.

making – is a law heavily influenced by the dominant legal models in circulation throughout much of the world. The law requires any group of people wishing to register a charity to provide to the Ministry of Civil Affairs an organizational charter and a statement specifying the composition and duties of its decision-making and operational bodies as well as ensuring it has sound financial and asset management systems, liquidation provisions, and other trappings of formal nonprofit organizations as would be commonly found outside China. Again, these are organizational and governance structures akin to many for-profit businesses. That is, the party-state has ensured that registering a legal civil society organization in China should not be a simple free-for-all comers process. A high degree of formality and disclosure is required, which ultimately makes for a more globally legitimized law but also one which subjects registrants to surveillance and control by a range of ever-vigilant state actors (Spires 2020).

At the same time as the organizational structures and practices mandated by the Charity Law are formal and recognizable to states everywhere, its political provisions ensure that successful applicants remain fundamentally conservative and supportive of the political status quo. Registering as a charity, for example, does not automatically allow a group to fundraise from the Chinese public. Only after two years of legal registration and "sound" operation – a never-defined term – can an organization apply for permission to publicly fundraise, at which point, of course, government actors can decide whether the group has been sufficiently faithful to the party-state to warrant such authorization. As with many Chinese laws, other clauses require that activities by registered groups must not violate social morality or national security, neither of which is defined. For feminist groups, LGBTQ groups, and others who may be interested in the promotion of and enforcement of basic social and political rights for marginal-ized populations, such vaguely worded admonitions serve as a warning to not cause trouble by making public claims or demands on the state. Whatever the international connections such groups have had in the past, and however influ-enced they may have been by ideas that came from outside China, the message of the Charity Law to domestic activists is that such actions will not be tolerated. The INGO Law, moreover, restricts foreign donors to supporting only legally registered organizations, cutting off what used to a reliable source of funding for some of China's most marginalized communities. Far from authorizing the rights-based activism promoted rhetorically by GCS actors, these sorts of restrictions provide a legal justification for disallowing legal registration and for punishing those that overstep the government's political red lines.

Whether we consider the funds that have flown from overseas to Chinese grantees, the training programs supported by foreign donors, or the regulatory models that have so heavily impacted the opportunities for domestic civil society actors to obtain legal status, it is ultimately unrealistic to view the inroads that the agents of GCS have made into China as simply another expression of economic neoliberalism. This is not to deny that insights from the broader scholarly literature are theoretically sound and likely appropriate for many other national contexts. But in the case of the world's largest authoritarian state, the political constraints shaping and confronting GCS actors in China loom largest. Against this backdrop, it may be more appropriate to view both funding flows and the thrust of foreign advice about civil society structures and regulation as well in tune with the Chinese party-state's own political and social agenda, offering lip service to democratization and human rights yet doing little to challenge the status quo in any radical way.

The Promise and Threat of Cosmopolitan Values

Within the political constraints imposed by a fearful authoritarian state, GCS's impact on China can be clearly seen in the development of globally recognizable charitable regulations, the foreign-designed organizational models promoted via "capacity-building" programs, and the relatively small amounts of funding directed toward grassroots NGOs. Yet, I would suggest that the main impact of GCS on China is to be found in the circulation of ideas – the notion of "universal values" and the implications of an independent, active, and critical civil society that so worried regime supporters like Zhou Benshun, Wang Shaoguang, and the authors of Document #9. Although much less visible, these ideas arguably hold many more far-reaching consequences for China.

The agents of GCS employ language that understandably worries adherents of a one-party authoritarian state. While commonly rendered in China (and elsewhere) as "universal values" (*pushi jiazhi*, in Chinese), the kinds of ideals and ideas embodied in this body of thinking have been well-articulated by political theorist David Held as "cosmopolitan" values. As Held put it, cosmopolitan values are:

> those basic values that set down standards or boundaries that no agent, whether a representative of a government, state, or civil association, should be able to cross. Focused on the claims of each person as an individual or as a member of humanity as a whole, these values espouse the idea that human beings are in a fundamental sense equal and that they deserve equal political treatment; that is, treatment based upon the equal care and consideration of their agency irrespective of the community in which they were born or brought up. (Held 2003, p. 514)

Acknowledging that these values could seem out of sync with a diverse world composed of independent nation-states, Held points out that "such values are already enshrined in, and central to, the laws of war, human rights law, and … many other international rules and legal arrangements" that have transformed – and arguably weakened – the Westphalian idea of inviolable state sovereignty (Held 2003, p. 514). Fundamentally concerned with human rights and democratic political processes, Held's articulation of cosmopolitan values is precisely the one that not only rankles authoritarians everywhere but also particularly worries leaders of one-party state's like China's, "for these are principles that are universally shared and can form the basis for the protection and nurturing of each person's equal interest in the determination of the institutions that govern his or her life" (Held 2003, p. 515).

The values and principles Held enumerates are ones that feature prominently in the rhetoric of liberal–democratic governments and the INGOs that call them home. Alongside the USA, European governments and organizations, for example, have played visible roles in promoting civil society and human rights in China. A number of German foundations have been active in China since the early 2000s, including Heinrich-Böll-Stiftung, Friedrich-Ebert-Stiftung (FES), and Konrad-Adenauer-Stiftung, all of which registered official representative offices after the INGO Law took effect. Sitting well within the GCS normative framing, FES, for example, works with Chinese government agencies and academics on issues like human rights, rule of law, and participatory governance.[13] Another European group active in supporting Chinese civil society and cosmopolitan values is the Danish Institute for Human Rights, which in 2018 launched a four-year program dedicated to promoting "civil, economic and social rights in China through a functioning legal system and effective access to justice for all," including helping Chinese primary and secondary schools implement a groundbreaking human rights educational curriculum.[14] European prize committees have publicly recognized the achieve-ments of Chinese activists, like public interest lawyer Guo Jianmei, who was awarded the Simone de Beauvoir Prize (France) in 2010 and the Right Livelihood Award (Sweden) in 2019.[15]

Greenpeace, arguably the world's most famous environmental activist group (headquartered in Amsterdam) offers a volunteer leadership training program "open to anyone, anywhere in the world who wants to organize, engage and take action against environmental destruction, climate change and social injustices. All we ask is that you are ready and willing to lead the change you want to see in the world."[16] World Vision, a Christian humanitarian aid organization based in

---

[13] https://china.fes.de/our-work/society-and-politics – Accessed August 31, 2023.

[14] www.humanrights.dk/where-we-work/china – Accessed August 31, 2023.

[15] Guo also won the International Women of Courage Award in 2011, given by the US State Department and presented to her by the then Secretary of State Hillary Clinton and First Lady Michelle Obama.

[16] www.greenpeace.org/international/act/volunteer-leadership-training/ – Accessed January 10, 2023.

the UK, aspires to promote "justice that seeks to change unjust structures affecting the poor among whom we work."[17] And Oxfam, a UK-originated organization with an active presence in Hong Kong, fights inequality in pursuit of "a world that is just and sustainable. A world in which people and planet are at the center of just economies. A world in which women and girls live free from gender-based violence and discrimination. Where the climate crisis is contained, and inclusive and accountable governance systems allow for those in power to be held to account."[18] Each of these organizations, like those US-based NGOs that have loomed so large in the imagination of critics and policymakers in Beijing, has been active in mainland China since at least the early 2000s and has maintained programs on the ground in China, even after the promulgation of the 2017 INGO Law.

Although Hong Kong-based and European groups have been active in China for years, within China the USA is often taken as the foil against which China's economy, society, and political system are measured and compared (although the wisdom of this is obviously questionable).[19] In her writing on Chinese soft power, political scientist Maria Repnikova notes that "throughout the discussions on motivations for soft power, it is evident that Chinese scholars largely respond to what they perceive as threats emanating from the West – the "West" often used as a synonym for the United States" (Repnikova 2022, p. 8). Just as the USA looms large in the Chinese imagination as the threat of "the West," it plays a similar role in Chinese perceptions of GCS and universal values. As the sole remaining superpower after the collapse of the Soviet Union, and undoubtedly the world's largest rhetorical promoter of democracy and civil society (and capitalism, of course), from Beijing's perspective it makes sense to focus on the USA when examining GCS intentions in China.

Linking the USA and GCS

In the mid 2000s, when the Color Revolutions first came on Beijing's radar, four prominent US-based donor organizations – some of which also ran programs supporting Chinese activists – publicly stated their support for what was becoming known as "universal values," and for civil society's active participation in China. Before turning to each specific case, it is important to recognize that the democratic political implications of NGO activity are highly touted not only by private donors

---

[17] www.worldvision.org/about-us/mission-statement – Accessed January 10, 2023.

[18] www.oxfam.org/en/what-we-do/about – Accessed January 10, 2023.

[19] A more extensive comparison of GCS actors hailing from different regions and countries is beyond the scope of this Element. I would expect to find more convergence than substantive difference in the China programs of European and American GCS actors, but this is a topic that deserves considered attention in future research.

but also in the broader official rhetoric of the US government. In 2006, Barry F. Lowenkron, Assistant Secretary for Democracy, Human Rights, and Labor at the US Department of State, argued for a strong causal connection between the strength of a country's NGOs and the strength of a country's democracy:

> Today, all across the globe, NGOs are helping to establish and strengthen democracy in three key ways: First, NGOs are working to establish aware-ness of and respect for the right of individuals to exercise freedoms of expression, assembly and association, which is crucial to participatory dem-ocracy. Second, NGOs are working to ensure that there is a level playing field upon which candidates for elective office can compete and that the entire elections process is free and fair. Third, NGOs are working to build and strengthen the rule of just laws and responsive and accountable institutions of government so that the rights of individuals are protected regardless of which persons or parties may be in office at any given time. (Lowenkron 2006)

The four funders highlighted here were chosen because together they help delineate the US presence in Chinese civil society and because they have attracted the attention of officials in Beijing concerned about the potential negative polit-ical impacts of foreign NGOs. They include one private foundation (the Ford Foundation), one US government-supported GONGO (the NED), one US gov-ernment agency (the State Department's Bureau of Democracy, Human Rights, and Labor), and one private-government hybrid (the Asia Foundation).[20]

In their annual reports, on their websites, and in other publications, these grantmakers each proclaim the importance of NGOs to their work around the globe, and in China specifically. According to its website in 2006, the US Department of State's Bureau of Democracy, Human Rights and Labor "leads the U.S. efforts to promote democracy, protect human rights and international religious freedom, and advance labor rights globally."[21] Through its Human Rights and Democracy Fund grants program, the agency supported "innovative programming designed to uphold democratic principles, support democratic institutions, promote human rights, and build civil society in countries and regions of the world that are geo-strategically critical to the U.S."[22] The Bureau's website homepage explained that democratization of other countries is a key aspect of the US national interest:

> Promoting freedom and democracy and protecting human rights around the world are central to U.S. foreign policy. . . . The United States supports those

---

[20] The Asia Foundation receives a majority of its funding from the US government but also receives substantial private contributions.

[21] DRL homepage, www.state.gov/g/drl/ – Accessed October. 24, 2006.

[22] US Department of State, Bureau of Democracy, Human Rights and Labor, Washington, DC, July 28, 2005 – Accessed September 17, 2006 via www.state.gov/g/drl/rls/50318.htm.

persons who long to live in freedom and under democratic governments that protect universally accepted human rights. . . . The United States is committed to working with democratic partners, international and regional organizations, non-governmental organizations, and engaged citizens to support those seeking freedom.[23]

As a US government agency, these goals have changed little over time, although by 2023 the mission statement had been revised to reflect broader aspirations for specific groups, including advancing "the rights and equity of members of marginalized racial, ethnic, and religious communities, indigenous persons, persons with disabilities, and LGBTQI+ persons."[24] In 2023, the Bureau's approach to its work is also little changed, at least rhetorically, and its parent organization, the US Department of State, continues to publish an annual report that is consistently critical of China's record on civil society, human rights, and democracy.

Although the Asia Foundation is registered as a nonprofit public charity in the USA, it was funded secretly by the US Central Intelligence Agency until the connection between the two was exposed in 1967.[25] Today the Asia Foundation operates on a combination of government and private funds. In 2005, just over 50 percent of its budget came from government-allocated funds.[26] To many US observers in Beijing, this reality validated in part the Chinese concern that US-based foundations and US government interests are intimately linked. The Asia Foundation's mission statement in 2006 held that "[t]he Asia Foundation is a non-profit, non-governmental organization committed to the development of a peaceful, prosperous, just, and open Asia-Pacific region."[27] In 2023, the attributes "just" and "open" had been removed from its list of desirable goals for the region.[28] In 2006, on the main webpage for its China operations, we learned that "[t]he Asia Foundation in China supports civil society organizations and government institutions to enhance popular empowerment while increasing government accountability. Through financial support, professional training, and technical assistance, The Asia Foundation supports legal reform, improved governance, development of the non-profit sector, and women's rights and opportunities."[29] By 2023, the division

---

[23] DRL homepage: www.state.gov/g/drl/ – Accessed November 12, 2006.

[24] DRL mission statement: www.state.gov/bureaus-offices/under-secretary-for-civilian-security-democracy-and-human-rights/bureau-of-democracy-human-rights-and-labor/ – Accessed January 10, 2023

[25] Document 176, "Memorandum From the Central Intelligence Agency to the 303 Committee/1/," at www.state.gov/r/pa/ho/frus/johnsonlb/x/9098.htm – Accessed October 28, 2006.

[26] Based on Form 990 filed with the IRS for fiscal year 2005.

[27] Asia Foundation, Overview, www.asiafoundation.org/About/overview.html – Accessed October 19, 2006.

[28] Asia Foundation, Overview, https://asiafoundation.org/about/ – Accessed January 9, 2023.

[29] Asia Foundation, China Overview, at www.asiafoundation.org/Locations/china.html – Accessed March 14, 2005.

describing its work in China had removed language about "rights," "popular empowerment," "government accountability," and "governance," although language about "civil society" and "gender equality" featured prominently.[30]

The Ford Foundation introduced itself in its 2005 Annual report as "a resource for innovative people and institutions worldwide. Our goals are to: Strengthen democratic values; Reduce poverty and injustice; Promote international cooperation; and Advance human achievement." To address the problems of the world, the Foundation said it aims "to encourage initiatives by those living and working closest to where problems are located; to promote collaboration among the nonprofit, government and business sectors; and to ensure participation by men and women from diverse communities and at all levels of society" (Ford Foundation 2005, p. 2). In its work in China, the values promoted by the Beijing office were said to include "a focus on poor and disadvantaged groups; an emphasis on participation as a core value that promotes community-based empowerment; a commitment to a rights approach; support for civil society; respect for diversity."[31] In pursuit of these values, Ford's China operations were charged with mobilizing "the creative potential of all of China's citizens, including those engaged in emerging non-government organizations, in meeting the challenges facing the country." In practical terms, the foundation said it "encourages cooperation among all sectors of society – grassroots organizations, NGOs, research centers, universities and government – in order to bring diverse perspectives to bear on a single set of problems."[32]

Almost twenty years later, in 2023, the foundation's mission statement remains similar to what it was when Hu Jintao had just ascended to power in China. The updated version explains that "we are guided by a vision of social justice – a world in which all individuals, communities, and peoples work toward the protection and full expression of their human rights; are active participants in the decisions that affect them; share equitably in the knowledge, wealth, and resources of society; and are free to achieve their full potential."[33] In line with this Element's own interest in China's "Going Out" (Section 3), in 2023, the Ford Foundation's Beijing office notes:

> Today, China is an important global actor with a presence in many of the regions where Ford operates. We now seek to work with Chinese academics,

---

[30] Asia Foundation, China Overview, at https://asiafoundation.org/where-we-work/china – Accessed January 9, 2023.

[31] Description found on Ford Foundation website at: www.fordfound.org/global/office/index.cfm? office=Beijing – Accessed October 20, 2006.

[32] Beijing office description, online at www.fordfound.org/global/office/index.cfm?office=Beijing – Accessed on October 20, 2006.

[33] Ford Foundation Mission Statement –www.fordfound.org/about/about-ford/mission/ – Accessed January 10, 2023.

policymakers, and nonprofits to ensure that China's impact in the world is equitable and sustainable. We also seek to strengthen the domestic ecosystem for philanthropy and impact investing to mobilize China's growing wealth for social good.[34]

Gone are explicit references to "grassroots," "NGOs," and seemingly a focus on working directly with groups inside China itself.

The NED, established in 1983 by the US Congress, in 2006 took as its mission "to strengthen democratic institutions throughout the world through private, non-governmental efforts."[35] In 1984, the organization, registered as a nonprofit yet funded by the US Congress and other US government agencies, began its China work by supporting the publication of *Chinese Intellectual*, a journal calling for democratic reforms in China. Also in the same year, three sociologists – Seymour Martin Lipset, Larry Diamond, and Juan Linz – launched the NED's first research project, "Democracy in Developing Nations."[36] Taking "opening dictatorial systems" as one of its main priorities, in 2002 the NED sought to press "the limits of what is possible – aiding groups working to create new openings, to defend democracy activists, to develop alternative channels for the flow of information, and to promote capacity development and democratic education within the democracy movement itself as well as the wider society."[37] In China, the NED said in 2002 that it had "conducted [a] diversified effort, aiding both internal programs to promote democratization, worker rights, and market reform; and external programs that defend human rights and provide access to independent ideas and information."[38] In a 2006 report prepared for the US Congress entitled "The Backlash Against Democracy Assistance," the head of the NED highlighted the importance of NGOs to democracy promotion in a range of countries, including China, and emphasized the NED's role in supporting NGO operations (Lugar 2006). In 2023, NED's rhetoric is little changed. Its self-presentation – available online to all, including party-state researchers in Beijing – declares that "NED is dedicated to fostering the growth of a wide range of democratic institutions abroad, including political parties, trade unions, free markets and business organizations, as well as the many elements of a vibrant civil society that ensure

---

[34] Ford Foundation China Overview –www.fordfound.org/our-work-around-the-world/china/ – Accessed January 10, 2023.

[35] NED, "Statement of Principles and Objectives," found online at www.ned.org/about/ principlesObjectives.html on September 19, 2006.

[36] "NED Twentieth Anniversary Timeline," found online at www.ned.org/about/nedTimeline.html on September 19, 2006.

[37] National Endowment for Democracy Strategy Document, 2002, pp. 5–6, www.ned.org/wp-content/uploads/2015/09/strategyDocument2002.pdf – Accessed January 10, 2023.

[38] National Endowment for Democracy Strategy Document, 2002, pp. 5–6, www.ned.org/wp-content/uploads/2015/09/strategyDocument2002.pdf – Accessed January 10, 2023.

human rights, an independent media, and the rule of law."[39] One of its China-focused grants in 2021 sought "to build the capacity of NGOs, support seasoned activists, and engage new activists, equipping them with skills to be effective human rights defenders and to reduce the risks they face in an increasingly repressive environment."[40]

While government agencies such as DRL and GONGOs like the NED are hardly representative of GCS – most analysts see them as arms of the US government – their language and rhetoric concerning civil society, rights, and democracy is strikingly similar to that of their unambiguously "private" coun-terparts like the Ford Foundation and hybrid groups like the Asia Foundation. That they are all US-based cannot justify dismissing them as "simply" repre-sentative of one country. Indeed, if we consider other major GCS actors headquartered elsewhere, we find quite similar rhetoric that fits well with David Held's articulation of a cosmopolitan, universal set of values common to humanity. Rhetoric is not always reality, of course, and the self-presentations of any of these four US-based groups or the others discussed here should not be taken at face value as automatically translating into support for radical, grass-roots NGOs seeking to change China's political system. Nonetheless, as seen from Beijing, their shared language about democracy, human rights, and civil society is implicitly and often explicitly and stridently critical of China and its one-party system.

Cosmopolitan Values at Work in Chinese Discourse

Despite the authoritarian state's explicit and systemic fear of political influence from abroad – and despite the scholarly criticism of GCS actors as agents of neoliberalism – GCS has effectively expanded political discourse and the recognition of human rights in China. This has been achieved not only through the literal introduction (and translation) of various terms (e.g., stakeholder and participation) but more importantly through legitimizing and supporting the recognition of marginalized voices. Examples here can be found in GCS work on women's rights, the rights of the disabled, drug users, sexual minorities, and – despite the horrors in Xinjiang that have earned condemnation from the United Nations (United Nations, 2022) – even ethnic minorities. To be sure, Xinjiang shows that there is much to be done to ensure basic human rights and accountability become a normal facet of life in China. But it is also clear that GCS has facilitated a pluralization of discourse in Chinese society, giving rise to a vocabulary that is rich in the language of cosmopolitan, universal values, and

---

[39] www.ned.org/about/ – Accessed January 10, 2023.
[40] www.ned.org/region/asia/mainland-china-2021/ – Accessed January 10, 2023.

to a repertoire of actions that promote those values and associated human rights. To give but a few examples, we can look at issues as varied as the performing arts, labor rights, and gender equality.

The 4th Beijing Nanluoguxiang Performing Arts Festival, held from May to July in the summer of 2013, brought together works from artists and theatre troupes from around mainland China, Hong Kong, Sweden, France, Germany, Israel, Hungary, the USA, Japan, and other places. Funded in cooperation with many non-PRC organizations – including the Taipei City Department of Cultural Affairs, the Hong Kong Arts Development Council, the Embassy of Sweden, and the Goethe Institut – the event even featured a three-day forum entitled "The Development of Nongovernmental Theatres in 10 Cities of China," expressly designed as "an attempt to discuss the relationship between theatre and the current social situation" (Penghao Theater 2013, p. 152). The festival was organized by Penghao Theater, a nonprofit theater space in Beijing that uses "Theater without Borders" as its English-language slogan. The theater, initiated by a Chinese dentist keen to rejuvenate the performing arts in China, has played host to performances of many styles. In his foreword to the 2013 Festival's program guide, Penghao founder Dr. Wang Xiang reflected on the state of the nation's soul and his aspirations for Chinese society:

> Government officials deal with crisis moronically, entrepreneurs pursue profits fanatically, the media acts hypocritically, average people turns [sic] to moronic entertainment, and even artists worship money and caters [sic] for moronic and vulgar interests. ... The reform and opening-up in 1978 unleashed massive economic potentials; however, opening the door of material desires without promoting political reform and resurrecting the national soul also brought about a blizzard of materialism and lust ...

> To preserve justice within a society, it takes laws and regulation, to preserve justice within the heart of individuals, it takes cognition of one's existence with a fulfilled heart, and a transcendent love for oneself, others, life and society. ... The real power of a nation could never be reflected in the provision of sufficient food and clothes to meet the basic animal instincts, a fictitious GDP number, or the self-claimed national confidence. A truly powerful nation would be able to endow its every citizen with the right live to like human beings and the right to experience and gain access to better lives; it would instill into its citizens intelligence, wisdom, spirit, character, creativity, diversity, nobleness, and artistic ability. (Penghao Theater 2013, p. 10)

Dr. Wang's bold critique of Chinese materialism and the failings of the government were printed in a publicly available, bilingual 176-page booklet detailing the dozens of events to be held during the festival. His invocation of concepts of justice, dignity, rights, and diversity stem in part, according to his own account, to the inspiration he received on his travels overseas. He observes – and laments – that after experimental theater was introduced to China from North America and Europe, it "soon lost its anti-commercial nature. And nothing remained of the anti-tradition, anti-mainstream and anti-authority character of the avant-garde theater. These assets should have been the pride of a nation through which we detect the problems in our society and thus make our society a better place" (Penghao Theater 2013, p. 9).

In the field of labor rights, a Chinese grassroots NGO called "Facilitator" began publishing in 2004 a series of short reflections, oral histories, and stories about rural-to-urban migrant workers. The exploitation and challenges faced by some 100 million (or more) such workers are now well-known in academic literature, but their suffering and struggles have not been well-reflected in economic, housing, and other policies that have powerful impacts over their lives. In the introduction to the first "Dagong Times" short volumes, Li Tao explains the need for such a publication, arguing that:

> In a society comprised of a diversity of classes, a group that has a firm grasp on discourse power (*huayu quan*) is a group that can voice out its class position, can pursue its class interests, and can participate in social policy-making. The size of discourse power depends on the strength of each group, but strength isn't a question of numbers; it's a question of whether people have the right to express their thoughts and needs. To be silent is to be overlooked. A just society is predicated on the establishment of a dialogue mechanism in which different classes are able to equally participate. . . . This is the motivation behind this book series: to allow the silent to speak, and to allow the helpless to help one another. (Li 2004, p. 4)

Again, we see the inherent commitment to democratic representation and participation, to dignity, to equality, and to freedom of thought and expression. Located in Beijing and embedded in the world of GCS actors in China through financial support and training programs, the language employed and the group's mission of service and empowerment to migrant workers is well-aligned with the express normative commitments of many INGOs.

In the field of gender equality, a number of activist-scholars in China have documented the multiple pathways through which foreign ideas about gender and (in)equality have impacted on Chinese women activists – and government practice – since the mid 1990s (Hsiung, Jaschok and Milwertz 2001). The 1995 United Nations Fourth World Conference on Women, held in Beijing, brought Chinese women's organizations like the Shaanxi Research Association for Women into dialogue with feminist NGOs from around the world. Founded in 1986, the association "initially defined itself as an organization to conduct and publicize academic research, but in the mid-1990s under the influence of the international feminist movement, its orientation shifted towards 'action research,' with the aim of promoting change in gender relations and gender equality at grass-roots level" (Gao 2010, p. 872). With support from the Ford Foundation, in 2002 longtime women's activist Gao Xiaoxian and her colleagues visited India to learn more about rural governance and gender there. Upon their return to China, they committed to conducting research and training to boost the numbers of women participating in the governance of China's rural villages. Working with four other organizations across China, including both grassroots NGOs and government agencies, with funding and assistance from the Ford Foundation in 2004, the Research Association began developing a series of training booklets for women village leaders. Their training materials, finished just in time for the 2008 village committee elections, introduced concepts such as "gender" (as opposed to biological sex) and gender roles, detailed examples of challenges faced by women village leaders in different parts of China, and discussed ways to "listen respectfully" (*lingting*) to the voices of women and how to represent their interests (Zhao, Du and Wen 2008). Despite the recent anti-feminist backlash in China (Huang 2023), thanks to people like Gao and her colleagues in the INGO community, gender equality remains on the agenda for Chinese civil society. In one example from 2022, a representative of the Chinese Association for NGOs called on the audience at the China Foundation Forum to help find ways to "mainstream" gender in the more than 900,000 officially registered NGOs in China, including thinking twice before reproducing gender stereotypes through their activities (Xu 2022).

Whether the actual operations or achievements of the specific organizations discussed here match their rhetorical commitments is an important question but not my focus here. Even in open, democratic societies with supportive traditions and laws, many nonprofit groups struggle to enact their ideals. Whatever failings or shortcoming these groups may have, it is important to recognize how they have embraced and promoted the "universal values" that are said to animate GCS. Those ideals link groups inside and outside China in intimate ways, building a community of shared values that transcends national boundaries, regardless of how any one group interprets, pursues, or implements them.

In this regard, GCS has made a difference in China, introducing key ideas supportive of universal values and providing legitimacy for Chinese civil society actors who seek to hold the Chinese state to account and to its own rhetorical aspirations to democracy and human rights. While those aspirations may be traced back to Communist ideals articulated prior to the PRC's establishment in 1949, intensive interactions with GCS since the 1980s have pushed the Chinese state to give substance to them, both to shore up domestic support and to project an image as a moral member of the international community.

Unfolding over a period of decades, this slow process has seen the realm of issues confronting China diversify. In early 2023, for example, Chinese representatives to the United Nations Human Rights Committee on Economic, Social and Cultural Rights (CESCR) found themselves bending over backward to argue that China protects the rights of LGBTQ people (United Nations Office n Geneva (UNOG), 2023), an issue unlikely to have been addressed by Beijing if it were not for the global rise in visibility and concern about LGBTQ rights in recent years. Recent censorship directives and personal experiences directly contradict the representatives' claims (Devlin and Ni 2017; Burton-Bradley 2022). Yet the very fact that the Chinese delegation was prepared to answer queries on the matter demonstrates that Beijing is keeping current with social issues arising internationally and is committed to at least learning the language and "what's expected" at such international forums. The groundwork for that 2023 performance was laid years earlier, arguably starting with the injection of funds dedicated to HIV-AIDs prevention and treatment provided to China by the Global Fund. Even though the Global Fund pulled out of China in apparent frustration at the state's refusal to incorporate true community-based organizations in its funding consultation models, it still popularized LGBTQ terminology and legitimated the idea of community-based organizations – concepts that resonated with LGBT groups, even as they experienced exclusion and sidelining from the Chinese state in practice.

The ideals and ideas about human rights and democracy that comprise GCS as a normative project may not be tangible, but they are realities that the Chinese party-state cannot restrict through legislation or surveille through bank account transfers from overseas donors. Ideas about freedoms and rights, as disembodied visions of an idealized future, can and have circulated within Chinese society even without active promotion by any clearly identifiable set of actors like NGOs or INGOs. They are concepts that resonate with the daily life experiences of millions of people who are discontent with the social, political, and economic status quo. Even when seemingly muddled or ill-defined, they are reinforced through repeated experiences and self-reflection, half-thought-through questioning or rigorous interrogation of harsh social realities. To be sure, the CCP has limited Chinese citizen's freedom of the press, the freedom of speech, assembly, religion, and a number of other basic rights that serve to nurture an open, democratic society. Yet as powerful as the CCP is, it cannot eliminate freedom of thought. People will take the ideas they encounter via GCS – and in the party-state's own lofty rhetoric – and do with them what they wish, even if that may not include taking immediate action to change their political circumstances.

3 State-Led Internationalization of (GO)NGOs

The ascension of Xi Jinping to the country's number one position in 2013 marked a turning point in the relationship of China and global civil society. No longer is China simply acted upon by foreign donors and INGOs. Now the Chinese state is increasingly taking an active part in contributing to – and perhaps seeking to reshape – what GCS is and does.

The contemporary "going out" of Chinese civil society – also understood as the internationalization of Chinese civil society, particularly GONGOs (Farid and Li 2021) – is largely a political project driven by the highest echelons of the Chinese party-state. Prior to public statements by the top leadership – Hu Jintao in late 2012 and Xi Jinping since then – there was little action to be found overseas by GONGOs or by China's homegrown grassroots groups. Although before 2013 there were occasional donations funneled through GONGOs and a handful of overseas projects developed by GONGOs, it was only after Xi's rise that Chinese state organs began to actively develop legal and administrative policies to support overseas activities. Over the past decade, the regulatory environment has grown and matured apace, with multiple agencies and ministries getting on board to support this new dimension of China's official soft power push. As such, the internationalization of Chinese nonprofits is an example of how clear, top-down directives can be quickly echoed and effected by state agents throughout China's political system, a phenomenon even more apparent and intense under Xi's administration. A series of new central government directives and speeches as well as policies at lower administrative levels now officially encourage Chinese GONGOs – and, rhetorically at least, Chinese grassroots NGOs – to venture abroad. We need to contextualize these developments in terms of Xi's BRI but also in terms of Beijing's broader effort to improve China's image overseas.

Entwining Economic and Social Ties Abroad

The rise of China in the past two decades and particularly since the global financial crisis of 2008 has invigorated academic investigations on the form, dynamics, and consequences of the arrival of new powers and the shifting of the unipolar system. With the spread of Confucius Institutes across the globe, the establishment of the Asian Infrastructure Investment Bank, and the BRI, many have suggested that the Chinese state is resolved to project its cultural influence and build institutional power through institutions of global governance (Vlassis 2016; Kennedy 2018; Kastner, Pearson and Rector 2018). While scholars may disagree on the effectiveness of these efforts, the drive to send Chinese nonprofits abroad is well in line with the broader economic policy emphasis and is evidenced most obviously by the explicit references to "governance" (*zhili*) used in official policy documents.

From a broader political perspective, state support for the "going out" of Chinese civil society groups is an extension of its support for the overseas expansion of Chinese enterprises. Despite being shunned and targeted with international sanctions after the violent suppression of the 1989 Tiananmen Movement, in 1990 the party's Eighth Five-Year Plan made plain the leadership's global economic ambitions, urging Chinese businesses – mostly state-owned enterprises (SOEs) at the time – "to consolidate existing markets and actively explore new ones" outside of China.[41] That was quickly followed in 1993 with official party promises to "grant qualified manufacturers and tech companies the right to operate foreign business."[42] In 1996, the then General Secretary Jiang Zemin, on a visit to Hebei, urged greater study of how to support the "going out" (*zou chuqu*) of Chinese SOEs into international markets.[43] Starting with a report by Premier Zhu Rongji in October 2000, these initial formulations of economic "going out" policies were formalized in a series of party-state proclamations and reports, sitting comfortably alongside preparations for China's long-sought admission to the WTO in 2001.[44] In 2012, as Hu Jintao was preparing to step down at the Party's 18th National Congress, he set the stage for a more people-focused narrative. Still hinting at the national economic interest underpinning the "going out" policy, Hu pledged that China would "take solid steps to promote

[41] Reformdata. 1990. "Recommendations of the Central Committee of the Communist Party of China on the Formulation of the Ten-Year Plan for National Economic and Social Development and the Eighth Five-Year Plan." www.reformdata.org/1990/1230/4152.shtml – Accessed October 27, 2022.

[42] Takungpao. 2013. "Decision of the Central Committee of the Communist Party of China on Several Issues Concerning the Establishment of a Socialist Market Economy System." http://news.takungpao.com/history/party/2013-11/2013005.html – Accessed November 1, 2022.

[43] Xinhua News. 2021. "100 Snapshots in 100 Years: 1996, 'Bringing in' and 'Going out' Strategies." www.news.cn/politics/2021-12/08/c_1211478976.htm – Accessed October 27, 2022.

[44] The State Council. 2000. "Proposal of the Central Committee of the Communist Party of China on the Formulation of the Tenth Five-Year Plan for National Economic and Social Development." www.gov.cn/gongbao/content/2000/content_60538.htm; The State Council. 2001. "On the National Economic and Social Development Outline of the Tenth Five-Year Plan." www.gov.cn/gongbao/content/2001/content_60693.htm; China News. 2002. "Building a Well-off Society in an All-round Way and Opening a New Page for Building Socialism with Chinese Characteristics." www.chinanews.com.cn/2002-11-17/26/244504.html; The Central People's Government of the People's Republic of China. 2007. "Accelerating the Pace of Reform, Opening Up and Modernization, and Seizing Greater Victory in the Cause of Socialism with Chinese Characteristics." www.gov.cn/test/2007-08/29/content_730511.htm – All accessed October 22, 2022.

public diplomacy as well as people-to-people and cultural exchanges, and protect China's legitimate rights and interests overseas."[45]

While "going out" in the economic realm may have been the brain child of Jiang Zemin and Zhu Rongji – or, behind the scenes, Deng Xiaoping – it was not until 2013 that newly installed General Secretary Xi Jinping consolidated the overseas expansion of Chinese businesses under the umbrella of the "Belt and Road Initiative." Announced in 2013, Xi's signature economic push presents a grand narrative of global prosperity through Chinese-led trade along multiple land routes and sea trade. Rhetorically, BRI hearkens back to the ancient days of the Silk Road linking Europe and Asia and, especially for Chinese audiences, the glory of the Ming Dynasty seafaring explorer Zheng He, said to have led a thousand ships into Southeast Asia and all the way to the eastern shores of Africa, bridging China and the world and bringing the world's treasures to the Middle Kingdom.

To be clear, there has been both skepticism and pushback against the BRI from local civil society in target investment countries. In Zambia, where the Bank of China has branches to facilitate, among other things, Chinese investment and construction in copper mining and a multibillion dollar hydroelectric plant, local politicians and civil society actors have been critical of Chinese practices on the ground. As one local civil society leader expressed in 2011, aside from secrecy and suspicious tax breaks: "There is a feeling among civil society that our government is working with the Chinese investors in order to loot our national resources for their benefit and not the benefit of the Zambian people" (Redvers 2011). China overtook the USA in 2009 as Africa's largest trading partner (Albert 2017), generating criticisms concerning labor rights, low transparency, and conflicts with local communities. Broader studies of local civil society responses are few and far between, but existing scholarly and journalistic accounts document similar conflicts in a range of investment countries from Africa to Asia to Latin America (Sautman and Yan 2014; Leslie 2016; Jalloh and Wan 2019; Shieh et al. 2021; Shipton and Dauvergne 2021).[46]

A Dozen National-Level Policy Steps in Under Ten Years

Following on from Hu's "people-to-people and cultural exchanges" pledge in 2012, and virtually in unison with Xi's inauguration of the BRI, Beijing began issuing calls for Chinese nonprofits to "go out" into the world, often explicitly

---

[45] China Daily. 2012. "Firmly March on the Path of Socialism with Chinese Characteristics and Strive to Complete the Building of Moderately Prosperous Society in All Respects." https://language.chinadaily.com.cn/19thcpcnationalcongress/2017-10/16/content_32684880_12.htm – Accessed October 25, 2022.

[46] The criticisms and concerns raised in these places will only be better understood by sustained and grounded study, which is outside the scope of this current analysis.

linking them to support for Chinese enterprises' international ventures. In the nine years from 2013 to 2021, central party leadership and institutions issued at least a dozen reports, white papers, statements, and administrative measures to reinforce the message and to facilitate the international ventures of Chinese nonprofits.

In a 2013 address to the Indonesian parliament, Xi Jinping argued that to increase mutual understanding and friendship between the two countries, they should "encourage more friendly exchanges between youth, think tanks, parliaments, NGOs and civil organizations."[47] Soon thereafter, in January 2014, the Ministry of Finance and the State Taxation Administration updated rules on tax exemptions for NGOs, no longer requiring that the scope of the organization's activities be primarily within China.[48] In 2014, the Ministry of Commerce issued trial "Measures for the Administration of Foreign Aid," listing overseas volunteering services among the projects that could be supported by official foreign aid funds.[49] Explicitly connecting the BRI and the going out of Chinese nonprofits, the following year the National Development and Reform Commission, Ministry of Foreign Affairs, and Ministry of Commerce jointly issued a paper entitled "Vision and Actions on Jointly Building Silk Road Economic Belt and 21st-Century Maritime Silk Road." In detailing its "cooperation priorities" (*hezuo zhongdian*), the statement urged all parties to "increase exchanges and cooperation between non-governmental organizations [*minjian zuzhi*] of countries along the Belt and Road, organize public interest activities concerning education, health care, poverty reduction, biodiversity and ecological protection for the benefit of the general public, and improve the production and living conditions of poverty-stricken areas along the Belt and Road."[50]

A major new initiative under the BRI rubric emerged in 2015, when Xi Jinping announced at the UN Development Summit in New York that China would establish a South–South Cooperation Assistance Fund, with an initial provision of US$2 billion, to support South–South cooperation and assist developing countries in implementing the 2030 Agenda for Sustainable

---

[47] ASEAN-China Centre. 2013. "Speech by Chinese President Xi Jinping to Indonesian Parliament." www.asean-china-center.org/english/2013-10/03/c_133062675.htm – Accessed October 28, 2022.

[48] Shuiwu. 2014. "Notice of the Ministry of Finance and the State Administration of Taxation on Issues Related to the management of Tax-Exempt Qualifications of Non-Profit Organizations." www.shui5.cn/article/9a/69498.html – Accessed October 28, 2022.

[49] Ministry of Commerce of the PRC. 2014. "Measures for the Administration of Foreign Aid (for Trial Implementation)." http://tfs.mofcom.gov.cn/article/ba/bi/201603/20160301285274.shtml – Accessed October 28, 2022.

[50] Belt and Road Forum for International Cooperation. 2017. "Vision and Actions on Jointly Building Silk Road Economic Belt and 21st-Century Maritime Silk Road." http://2017.beltandroadforum.org/n100/2017/0407/c27-22.html – Accessed October 28, 2022.

Development.[51] The following year, China's Ministry of Commerce sought comments on its draft plans to implement the Fund, explicitly incorporating "social organizations" as eligible applicants and implementors.[52] The link between BRI and the "going out" of Chinese NGOs was reinforced again in 2016, when the General Office of the CPC Central Committee and the General Office of the State Council proposed that the government should "guide domestic social organizations step by step to carry out overseas exchange programs, join international non-governmental organizations ... play a supporting and supplementary role in foreign economic, cultural, scientific and technological, educational, and environmental protection exchanges, and act as an important platform in people-to-people communication between China and other countries." Of course, as would be expected given the tight controls over Chinese civil society, the joint opinion paper further mandated that Chinese groups wishing to operate overseas branches "must obtain approval from their professional supervisory units or the units responsible for the management of their foreign affairs."[53]

In 2017, China injected an additional US$1 billion in funding into the South–South Fund, and, by the end of that year, the Fund claimed that "China had signed cooperation agreements with 15 international organizations ... and had implemented nearly 200 development cooperation projects in 27 countries and regions ... [covering] food safety, post-disaster reconstruction, refugee relief, medical treatment and public health, maternal and child health, poverty alleviation, education and training, and trade and investment facilitation," benefiting "about 5 million people in developing countries."[54]

In 2018, the Chinese government established the China International Development Cooperation Agency (CIDCA), a new agency intended to integrate the functions of the Ministry of Commerce for foreign aid work and the functions of the Ministry of Foreign Affairs for foreign aid

---

[51] China International Development Cooperation Agency. 2018. "A Brief Introduction of the South-South Cooperation Assistance Fund." www.cidca.gov.cn/2018-08/24/c_129939202.htm – Accessed October 28, 2022.

[52] Ministry of Commerce of the PRC. 2016. "Measures for the Application and Management of the South-South Cooperation Assistance Fund Projects (for Trial Implementation)." http://tfs.mofcom.gov.cn/article/as/201609/20160901387579.shtml – Accessed October 28, 2022.

[53] The National People's Congress of the PRC. 2016. "Opinions on Reforming the Regulation System of Social Organizations and Promoting the Healthy and Orderly Development of Social Organizations." www.npc.gov.cn/npc/c30280/201609/5a8325a3b75443a489c982cb62e560a5.shtml – Accessed October 28, 2022.

[54] China International Development Cooperation Agency. 2018b. "An Introduction of the South-South Cooperation Assistance Fund." http://en.cidca.gov.cn/2018-08/20/c_264437.htm – Accessed October 28, 2022.

coordination.[55] Its responsibilities are "to formulate strategic guidelines, plans and policies for foreign aid, coordinate and offer advice on major foreign aid issues, advance the country's reforms in matters involving foreign aid, and identify major programs and supervise and evaluate their implementation."[56] Institutionally, CIDCA will likely become a major player – or perhaps the single most important official player – in coordinating the "going out" of Chinese nonprofits.

Reflecting Xi Jinping's focus on strengthening China's influence in the world, the onset of the global COVID-19 pandemic in early 2020 did not diminish the "going out" policy push. To the contrary, the pandemic offered China an opportunity to support other countries experiencing high infection and death rates by donating medical supplies and providing its homegrown vaccine to people in need. Following an earlier set of separate measures and pronouncements, in 2021 the Ministry of Commerce, the Ministry of Foreign Affairs, and CIDCA jointly issued a set of "Measures for the Administration of Foreign Aid." These *Measures* expanded the types of aid projects available under official aid programs to include medical team projects, emergent humanitarian projects, and the South–South Cooperation Assistance Fund projects. Significantly, the *Measures* explicitly state that the South–South Fund can be used to finance aid projects carried out by "international organizations, social organizations, and think tanks," providing additional legal support for government funds to financially support nonprofit internationalization efforts.[57]

Two other major steps taken in 2021 indicate Beijing's continued interest in supporting the "going out" of Chinese "social organizations" (*shehui zuzhi*), despite the numerous challenges posed by the pandemic. First, in January 2021, the State Council issued a white paper, *China's International Development Cooperation in the New Era*, pledging that China will "work for a more equitable and balanced global development partnership." To achieve this, China will "encourage the private sector, NGOs and social groups, and charitable organizations to play a greater role" by continuing "to improve relevant laws, regulations and institutions, providing a legal guarantee for international development cooperation." Reflecting the increased political desire for centralization of authority and coordination, the paper further states that "the inter-ministerial coordination mechanism for foreign aid will play a more active role,

---

[55] People's Daily. 2018. "The International Development Cooperation Agency was Founded Today and Becomes a Business Card to Showcase China's New Responsibility." http://world.people.com.cn/n1/2018/0418/c1002-29934894.html – Accessed October 31, 2022.

[56] China International Development Cooperation Agency. 2018c. "What We Do." http://en.cidca.gov.cn/2018-08/01/c_259525.htm – Accessed October 31, 2022.

[57] China International Development Cooperation Agency. 2021. "Measures for the Administration of Foreign Aid." www.cidca.gov.cn/2021-08/31/c_1211351312.htm – Accessed October 28, 2022.

and we will forge synergy at all levels, coordinate efforts by central departments, local governments and social organizations, pool premium resources, and enhance cohesion and efficiency."[58]

The second major pronouncement of support came in September 2021, when the Ministry of Civil Affairs (MOCA) – the ministry in charge of overseeing domestic nonprofits – issued the "14th Five-Year Plan for the Development of Social Organizations." This document explicitly states that the Ministry will "steadily facilitate the 'Going Out' of domestic social organizations, carry out overseas cooperation in an orderly manner, enhance the ability of China's social organizations in the participation of global governance, and improve the influence of Chinese culture and China's 'soft power'."[59] The reference to participating in "global governance" aligns well with China's increasing efforts to shift the center of international human rights debates at the United Nations in order to better accord with Beijing's emphasis on social and economic rights over political and civil rights (Zhang and Buzan 2020). Not by coincidence, some of the same officials in charge of charity issues at MOCA have also participated in China's human rights engagement and reporting at the United Nations in Geneva and New York. Similarly, the rhetorical support for China's "soft power" initiatives also smartly echoes Xi Jinping's calls to "increase China's soft power, give a good Chinese narrative, and better communicate China's messages to the world" (Shambaugh 2015, p. 99).

Merging Domestic and International "Charity" Practices

The tying together of domestic charity promotion efforts with international practices is another aspect of how China continues to "link up with the international track" outside the economic realm. September in China has a special significance in terms of charity and philanthropy. September 9 is the day on which Tencent hosts its annual "Tencent 99 Giving Day," when China's one billion WeChat users can make donations of any size to a large range of charitable causes. September also has special significance in official circles, as September 5 has been designated by MOCA as "China Charity Day," on which provincial and lower level MOCA offices are expected to promote charitable events and spread awareness of philanthropy, volunteering, and serving the needy. In 2022, MOCA's theme for China Charity Day was

---

[58] The State Council. 2021a. "Full Text: China's International Development Cooperation in the New Era." https://english.www.gov.cn/archive/whitepaper/202101/10/content_WS5ffa6bbb c6d0f72576943922.html – Accessed November 1, 2022.

[59] The State Council. 2021b. "The Ministry of Civil Affairs on the Issuance of the '14th Five-Year Plan' for the Development of Social Organizations." www.gov.cn/zhengce/zhengceku/2021-10/08/content_5641453.htm – Accessed October 31, 2022.

"going forward hand in hand to do charity, spreading the true, the good, and the beautiful (*xieshou zuo cishan, chuanbo zhenshanmei*)," which was inspired by Xi Jinping's recent call to "serve as an example by positively promoting the true, the good, and the beautiful, spreading positive energy, mobilizing others to move upwards towards charity (*xiangshang xiangshan*), and promoting core socialist values, all with the goal of realizing the rejuvenation of the great Chinese nation by contributing one's light and passion."[60]

While September's activities allow the central government ministry (MOCA) a chance to amplify the central leader's messages on charity, goodwill, and patriotism within China, they also connect Chinese charities to the outside world. September 5 was designated as "China Charity Day" to match the UN's International Day of Charity. The UN designated that day as such to memorialize Mother Teresa, the missionary nun who was awarded the 1979 Nobel Peace Prize for her efforts to combat poverty and alleviate suffering in India. Even though it may not be frequently acknowledged or widely understood as such within China itself, this intentional connection is another example of how GCS and global humanitarianism have impacted China. It also reinforces the Chinese government's efforts to be regarded domestically and abroad as a responsible and caring member of the international humanitarian community.

Experiences and Forms of "Going Out"

The series of policy announcements and measures surveyed in the previous sections are clearly designed to facilitate the internationalization of Chinese civil society. Although interrupted by the COVID-19 pandemic starting in early 2020, as restrictions are lifted and China works to reengage with the outside world we should expect these policies to be implemented more widely. In political terms, they are paramount both internally and externally to help explain and justify additional investments in overseas projects and an expanded overseas presence for Chinese GONGOs. They also provide domestic political legitimacy and rhetorical support for grassroots Chinese groups seeking to engage overseas.

Prior to these supportive measures, the possibilities for going out were much more limited. In 2014, a former PRC government official then working at an environmental protection INGO was keen to "go out." His group had become "indigenized" (*bentuhua*), he said, thanks to a massive influx of domestic

---

[60] Ministry of Civil Affairs. 2022. "Minzhengbu bangongting guanyu zuohao diqige 'Zhonghua cishan ri' youguan gongzuo de tongzhi." "民政部办公厅关于做好第七个"中华慈善日"有关工作的通知. www.mca.gov.cn/article/xw/tzgg/202208/20220800043506.shtml – Accessed November 1, 2022.

financial support and an almost fully Chinese-led staff and advisory board. During a conversation at the group's Yunnan office, he argued that government policies were outdated:

> I feel their policies are ancient (*gulao*). We should be able to raise funds in China and use them in China or overseas, in third-world countries where there's need. ... With globalization, this is a trend. There's great need along the Mekong, in Burma, or Laos, or other countries in Asia. The ecological environment is shared. I hope the government revises the regulations to let us call ourselves "international," like "Conservation International" or something like "Clean Earth." Then we could go out to wherever the need is.

The policy changes outlined above might have improved the possibilities for groups with aspirations like his, but if the political backdrop offers both motivation and legitimacy for the internationalization of Chinese civil society, what has been the response of civil society actors charged (or moved) to heed the call to go out? Developments in recent years compel us to disentangle understandings of "China" as the Chinese state and "China" as bottom-up actors, including "indigenized" INGOs run by Chinese staff, domestic grassroots organizations, and a youthful Chinese diaspora engaging in social issues outside the country's borders. Study abroad, the growing wealth of Chinese private business owners, and increasing exposure to notions of human rights and freedoms are all factors that complicate the in/out dichotomy often used (including by this author) when thinking about GCS and China. Although the scale of "going out" has been small to date, there are some intriguing examples of the ways in which Chinese civil society actors are working overseas. The rise of diverse diasporic activism complicates the picture even further, with some organizations targeting change in China and others seeking to change the world outside China itself, acting as full and equal participants within GCS and upholding the universal values and norms often attributed to it.

Small in Scale, but Increasing

Given the CCP's guarded stance on survey data collection domestically, the general political sensitivity of Chinese civil society as a topic of research, and the lack of transparency in many government processes and statistics, conducting broad surveys of Chinese civil society organizations is rife with challenges. As with efforts to ascertain the scale of domestic civil society and INGOs in China, information on the scale of Chinese NGOs' overseas activity is also limited. However, there are at present two public databases collating information on Chinese NGOs and GONGOs that have been involved in going out. The China Development Brief (CDB) maintains an online list of overseas projects, listing sixty-two such projects in twenty-three countries as of April 2023. Their bilingual mapping includes activities of both GONGOs and grassroots NGOs and lists, for example, fifteen ongoing or completed projects in Nepal and eleven in Myanmar, and projects ranging from a clean water project in Nigeria to Chinese language teaching in northern Thailand (China Development Brief 2023). While limited in scope, the CDB database provides enough detail on the activities and organizations involved to depict a varied tapestry of projects across a range of societies from Africa to Southeast Asia.

The much larger Chinese NGO Internationalization Database, created by Ying Wang, a PhD candidate at Leiden University, collates data on Chinese humanitarian and development assistance projects culled from NGO and GONGO websites, news reports, and other public sources. Stretching from 2005 through 2020, this database includes details on 700 distinct donations and projects operated by over 100 NGOs (including GONGOs) in over 100 countries worldwide. From Wang's efforts, we can see that the scope of activities is quite broad, although deeper analysis is frustrated by a lack of uniformity in public source reporting on activities and funding flows.

As the CDB's and Wang's databases indicate, the overseas operations of Chinese NGOs and GONGOs are broad in scope and varying in scale (Li and Dong 2018; Zou and Jones 2020). What Chinese NGOs are actually doing in various regions of the world is an open question, however. Existing research has mostly focused on Africa (Brenner 2012; Hsu, Hildebrandt, and Hasmath 2016) or on single-country studies (Lu and Peng 2018; Zou and Jones 2020). It generally indicates, however, that the Chinese government has encouraged and supported Chinese NGOs' presence and practices in Africa and in neighboring countries like Myanmar, for example, to safeguard the country's overseas economic interests. But with limited data, the medium- and longer-term impacts of Chinese NGO projects overseas remain unclear.

Straddling Two Civil Society Ecosystems

Statements from the Chinese government suggest that encouraging Chinese nonprofits to "go out" is now a vital part of China's official push for soft power influence and a key component of its "people-to-people" diplomatic strategy. Yet, to what extent this is mostly aspirational or actually supported by government resources is an open question. Looking at what Chinese groups that have gone out do and say about their motivations is one way to understand the interplay between government priorities, these groups' own bottom-up ambitions, and the larger GCS field in which they find themselves when leaving China's borders.

One example can be found in that of the Peaceland Foundation, a nonprofit formally registered in 2018 in Beijing that describes itself (in English) as "an international non-profit organization delivering emergence [sic] responses and long-term educational programs in global humanitarian crisis and environmental challenges."[61] Peaceland's self-description of a project on anti-poaching in Zimbabwe makes clear how it ties its work together with an effort to improve China's image overseas:

> African elephants are on the path to extinction in the next 50 years due to illegal poaching for ivory. Following its economic rise, China has become the world's largest ivory market and this has negatively led the Chinese to be labeled as the culprits of illegal poaching internationally. To change this false impression, the Peaceland Foundation initiated the Anti-Poaching Voluntary Operation in Africa. This is not just a volunteering campaign, but also our contribution to Chinese diplomacy.[62]

While this patriotic language might invite skepticism overseas as simply flag-waving for Beijing, Peaceland has also engaged in more traditional humanitarian relief work without the same explicit nod to Chinese diplomacy, including landmine clearing work in Cambodia, assistance for Syrian refugees in Lebanon, and relief for flood victims in Iran. It has joined the ranks of a very small number of Chinese homegrown NGOs with offices outside China, including in Lebanon, Zimbabwe, and Cambodia. Founded by an entrepreneur, according to its annual reports it has received no direct government subsidies since its establishment, although it has received funding from GONGOs like the China Social Assistance Foundation, the China Social Welfare Foundation, and the Chinese Red Cross Foundation, in addition to donations from private businesses.[63] In 2022, it was awarded official partnership status by UNESCO, the only Chinese foundation to enjoy that position.[64]

Rhetorically, groups like Peaceland walk in two worlds. The English version of Peaceland's public website evinces many of the same cosmopolitan values that inform the self-understandings of non-Chinese GCS actors: "With respect for different cultures, we have worked in 23 countries. The protection of

---

[61] Peaceland. [Undated]. "Introduction." http://en.peaceland.org.cn/introduction/ – Accessed November 2, 2022.

[62] China Development Brief. [Undated]. "Project Introduction – Anti-Poaching Operation in Zimbabwe." https://chinadevelopmentbrief.org/projects/anti-poaching-operation-in-zimbabwe/ – Accessed November 2, 2022.

[63] See details (in Chinese) at www.peaceland.org.cn/information/annual.

[64] UNESCO. 2022. "List of Foundations and similar institutions in official relations with UNESCO within the framework of the Directives concerning UNESCO official relations with foundations and similar institutions (29 C / Res. 64)." https://en.unesco.org/sites/default/files/list_foundations_official_relations_unesco.pdf – Accessed November 2, 2022.

vulnerable groups and the enhancement of local sustainable development are at the heart of all our missions."[65] In Chinese, meanwhile, its "vision" (*yuanjing*) statement replicates Beijing's official narrative about the motivations for going out, including "innovating global governance" (*chuangxin quanqiu zhili*).[66] I do not aim here to drill down into Peaceland's objectives, motivations, or impacts in the countries where it works. Rather, I highlight it as an example of how China is home to at least a small number of NGOs with an explicit international orientation that are well-versed in both the language of GCS and the language of the Chinese party-state. In employing language the state has already endorsed, this group joins the many Chinese civil society organizations who have long found it politically useful to borrow the language of the state when presenting their work and goals within China (Keech-Marx 2008; Spires 2011a; Leggett 2017). But Peaceland's relatively skillful straddling of two civil society ecosystems reveals a sophistication that is bound to become more common – and necessary – as more Chinese NGOs seek ways to "go out" into the world.

GCS's impact on Peaceland is also apparent in another easily overlooked but still consequential way. It's public Chinese-language website includes statements of its vision (*yuanjing*), mission (*shiming*), strategy (*zhanlüe*), and values (*jiazhiguan*), all elements of a "professional" NGO that have been promoted and nurtured in China through years of training programs originating in North America (Spires 2012). Fitting well into a globally standardized model of NGO structures and styles, this sort of self-presentation helps signal legitimacy outside of China (similar language appears on its English site). Inside China, it also reassures the government and the public that it is a trustworthy and capable organization well-positioned to pursue its declared goals.

Another relatively new organization is equally revealing in how it points to a possible future for bottom-up, people-to-people ties emerging from a new generation of Chinese young people. China House, a Shanghai-based "social enterprise" aimed at promoting young Chinese people's pursuit of the Sustainable Development Goals, is the brainchild of Hongxiang Huang, a Chinese national who obtained an MPA in Development Practice from Columbia University in 2013. During his studies at Columbia, Huang spent time in Latin America researching the social impacts of Chinese investments, an experience that inspired him to continue looking at the challenges of development and seeking ways to both raise awareness in China and to involve Chinese youth in sustainable development work. Since founding the group in 2014, he

---

[65] Peaceland. [Undated]. Introduction. en.peaceland.org.cn/introduction/ – Accessed November 2, 2022.

[66] Peaceland. [Undated]. Jigou Jieshao. www.peaceland.org.cn/introduction/ – Accessed November 2, 2022.

and his team have engaged over 2,000 Chinese young people in development projects, working in 27 countries alongside over 100 NGOs and multinational enterprises.[67] Their work has involved a range of environmental and social issues, including the illegal ivory trade in Africa, orangutan rescue in Indonesia, and helping Masai girls combat female genital mutilation in Kenya.

China House's self-presentation is well in line with the normative vision laid out by many scholars of GCS (e.g., Jordan 2011). Its English mission statement is "[t]o cultivate global vision, global competence, and global citizenship in young Chinese," while its vision statement centers on an aspiration to "build a bridge for communication and partnership between China and the rest of the world." Its explicitly outward-focused orientation distinguishes China House from grassroots groups that work to address China's domestic social issues and needs (Spires 2011a). Unlike those, its core work focuses on China *in* the world: "We conduct research and projects in collaboration with governments, NGOs, academic institutions and enterprises, to help China integrate into global sustainable development."[68] The group's "Who We Are" page features a photo of smiling young people wearing white T-shirts with "Chinese Global Citizens" emblazoned in English on the front. Standing on a grassy patch somewhere in rural Africa, they are holding aloft a China House-branded banner that reads, "See the world, make it better" in English. In Chinese, the much longer slogan reads, "Helping Chinese Youth Go into the World, Building the Dream of One Belt One Road." As with the Peaceland Foundation, pairing the language of GCS with Chinese government slogans reveals how groups like these seek to participate in global conversations while also assuring Beijing that their work fits well into the goals and vision of the Chinese party-state itself.

The straddling of these two civil society ecosystems should not by itself invite skepticism or cynicism about either Peaceland's or China House's "real" goals and work. Rather, as with established INGOs around the world, Chinese groups like these speak to a domestic audience to obtain legitimacy, legality, and support, while also engaging overseas peers and interlocutors in the language of a much more "global" civil society. Both groups represent a future in which Chinese wealth and the energy and enthusiasm of its people may be put to good use addressing globally recognized problems of poverty, development, climate change, and a host of other issues. As Chinese wealth continues to grow, we should expect that an increasing number of Chinese volunteers and philanthropists will take interest in overseas work, whether due to government pressures or their own personal concerns about development, environmental, or

---

[67] China House. 2022. (Home page.) www.globalchinahouse.com – Accessed November 5, 2022.

[68] China House. 2022. "Who We Are." www.globalchinahouse.com/who-we-are – Accessed November 4, 2022.

humanitarian issues. As such groups' influence and visibility overseas grows, we should also expect that the Chinese state will seek to monitor (if not outright control) and influence their work to ensure it aligns with Beijing's preferred narratives. At this point, it is unclear how much influence groups like these and others have on China's overseas image. While they may borrow BRI policies for rhetorical support, there is currently no official mechanism for BRI "branding" of Chinese civil society groups that go out. From the state's standpoint, whatever goodwill they can bring to China is welcome, but there is likely too much risk in granting their overseas work any sort of official stamp of approval until stricter monitoring and oversight mechanisms can be developed and implemented.

Groups like China House are significant for what they reveal about changes in the composition of GCS but also for what they reveal about generational change and aspirations within China itself. Much ado has been made in the USA, Australia, and elsewhere in the democratic world about the phenomenon of Chinese students studying abroad – often with more heat than light generated in the popular press – but it is already clear that some Chinese students who pursue overseas study are returning to China and seeking ways to bridge their compatriots and the outside world. As the China House T-shirts read, some people in this younger generation already see themselves as "Chinese global citizens." This self-identification process may continue to unfold as more young people travel and study overseas (Martin 2022), and as they reflect on what they perceive as gaps and commonalities between China and "the rest" of the world. Indeed, China House is not alone in this category of returnees working in civil society in China. Other groups have been founded by returnees from the USA, Australia, Europe, and elsewhere and work on issues as diverse as education for marginalized children, climate change, and migrant workers' rights.

None of this means, of course, that outward-focused groups like Peaceland and China House are "the norm" in China. To the contrary, all evidence actually points to them as unusual exceptions in the current world of Chinese civil society. But the longer-term domestic and global political and economic dynamics that have allowed such groups to develop continue to unfold, albeit not entirely smoothly due to disruptions like the COVID-19 pandemic. As already argued, the CCP's own emphasis on the "core socialist values" of democracy, freedom, and equality offers rhetorical support and inspiration to Chinese people who hold a "global citizen" orientation and want to put their values into action. Even with shifts (or freezes) in leadership at the top, China's overarching embrace of modernity means that the "universal values" so maligned by some conservative Chinese intellectuals are nearly impossible to extricate from the larger political and economic project that China has pursued for the last century and more. For at least a portion of the Chinese population, these larger trends will continue to inspire action grounded in the humanitarian and democratic principles that underpin much of GCS today.

Diaspora Activism – Multiple Meanings in a New Era

Although much existing literature – and much of my own work – frames work on GCS as organizations "going in" to China or Chinese groups "going out" to the rest of the world, the increasingly large numbers of Chinese young people studying abroad, Chinese migration to other countries, and globalization more broadly have provided for the emergence of at least two other conceptually distinct forms of "Chinese" participation in GCS. One, commonly referred to as "diaspora activism," is especially visible today thanks to social media, but it has a much longer history than the companies that encourage users to vie for eyeballs and "likes." Diaspora activism further complicates an originally some-what simpler image of GCS "in" China. Not only about political exiles or dissidents who have moved permanently abroad, diaspora activism today includes Chinese people living overseas who are deeply involved in searching for solutions to problems in their local communities. It includes people who are interested in improving transnational linkages to support activists in China, as well as more temporary exiles from Chinese civil society who aim to return home to resume their work after a period of "rest" overseas. In contrast to the more traditional conceptualization of diaspora activism, in the passages to come I also consider the experiences of people based outside China who work to ameliorate the economic, societal, and environmental impacts of Chinese investment in other countries. This latter group and its attendant form of activism – what one activist referred to in 2023 as "China in the world," as distinct from a "going out" of Chinese NGOs – is arguably a much newer development.

The most famous and arguably consequential example of Chinese diaspora activism stretches back to the turn of the twentieth century, when mostly ethnic Han intellectuals studying and living outside of the Qing's dynastic borders sought to introduce democracy and throw off the shackles of "foreign" Manchu imperial rule. Despite many failed attempts, years of organizing among like-minded elites outside (and inside) Qing territory eventually met with success in the 1911 Republican Revolution. Alongside a long list of now-revered revolutionaries, Dr. Sun Yat-sen, who studied in Hawaii and the British colony of Hong Kong, is heralded in official PRC textbooks as the "father of modern China" and memorialized at numerous sites across China.

Moving forward in time, the pro-democracy protests of the late 1970s, the student-initiated Tiananmen protest movement of 1989, and the repression of Falungong gave rise to another wave of overseas-based diasporic activism (Yang 2003; Junker 2019). Following the brutal suppression of those gathered in Tiananmen Square in June 1989 in particular, a few of the more prominent leaders of this period fled mainland China and found themselves in effective exile in the USA, Europe, Australia, Hong Kong, or Taiwan. Some sought to continue voicing the criticism of the PRC government that had motivated their initial participation but struggled to make lives for themselves outside their homeland (Chen 2012).

With increasing restrictions on Chinese civil society in the final years of the Hu-Wen government continuing into the Xi era (Yuen 2015), a number of activists have felt their lives and work to be so threatened that few choices remained but to seek refuge in other countries, at least for some period of time. Among the more famous of these is Dr. Wan Yanhai, an HIV-AIDS activist who left for the USA in 2010 out of concern that his NGO would be declared illegal and his family would suffer (Richburg 2010). Another activist, Lu Jun, co-founded Beijing Yirenping Center, an organization to combat health- and gender-related discrimination in China, which he ran for over ten years before it was shut under government pressure, pushing him into self-exile in the USA (Lu 2021). In the last few years, more than a few other activists from various fields have followed these examples and headed overseas. Some intend to remain overseas indefinitely as long as work and other circumstances permit, while others are keen to return to China to continue their activism when the situation allows. As one of these activists-in-exile explained to me in early 2023, one key distinction that should be made between this more recent cohort of activists who have left China and those from earlier eras – particularly the Tiananmen generation – is that this newer cohort emerged at a time of optimistic and continuous engagement *within* China on social issues. They had "come up through the trenches" of activism, learning invaluable lessons in collaboration with like-minded others whom they met inside NGOs and other civil society settings. They are not "one-off," highly individualized activists who got swept up in a moment of revolutionary fervor. Rather, they see their years of hard work within Chinese civil society as an invaluable wealth of experience that can still be put to effective use in China when they go home. Whether – and how – such a distinction continues to be relevant as time passes remains to be seen, but at least some of these more recent emigres intend to return to China.

Most of those activists who have left China more recently have found temporary homes in open democracies like the USA, Europe, and Australia. Exposure to life in democratic societies – through study, exchanges, or temporary self-imposed exile, in this case – can have many implications and consequences. Some seek to continue their activism through participating in local social movements. There is far from sufficient research in this area to generalize about the experience of this particular group, but a study by sociologist Mengyang Zhao (2021) points to the complexity of transnational activism and social movement learning. Zhao interviewed nineteen activists living in the USA and Europe, who were "involved in labor, feminist, LGBTQ, and human rights activism in China" recently, including "many [who] had the experiences of being harassed or detained by the authorities for their work" (Zhao 2021, p. 286). As Zhao argues, their experiences distinguish them from their peers in China and overseas, for "as politically engaged sojourners and immigrants, diaspora activists participate in a wide range of local activism, including those not directly pertaining to their home country politics. Such participatory experiences equip them with new perspectives on democracy, resistance, and international solidarity" (Zhao 2021, p. 282).

This is not to say that the "new perspectives" activists adopt are necessarily all laudatory of movements in liberal democratic settings, and Zhao carefully documents two broad critiques of what they observe, namely, the "over-institutionalization of social movements, and the discrepancy between social movement discourse and action" (Zhao 2021, p. 287). For some of the Chinese activists she studied, the relative ease with which activists in democracies pursued social change goals seemed to diminish the meaningfulness of their work. Locals' lack of understanding of the challenges facing activists in China also made transnational solidarity feel like an elusive ideal and contributed to a sense of disillusionment. Like many studies of GCS's impacts on China, such responses illuminate gaps between the lived experience of Chinese activists and that of their foreign counterparts. While not negating the potential for borrowing and learning from foreign experiences, the disillusionment of these activists points out the persistent need for Chinese activists to devise their own solutions to Chinese problems. As Zhao concludes:

> Although activists still believe and cherish the value of activism in challenging the status quo regardless of contexts, they start to doubt the meaning and feasibility of transnationalism when the organizing principle of most social movements is still strictly confined to the local level. Their aspiration for a more cosmopolitan world is crushed after gaining a better understanding of how the majority of social movements work in liberal democracies (Zhao 2021, p. 291).

Her sobering assessment of these activists' experience is not the end of the story, however. The creativity and perseverance this group of activists has demonstrated over the years in China suggest that they are likely to find ways to adapt lessons learned abroad to reinvigorate their work once they return to China.

Activating Chinese Activists

Diaspora activism should not be understood only as activists in exile. The concept can also be extended to people who find their way into activism only after moving overseas. Most obvious among these are Chinese youth who go abroad for undergraduate or postgraduate study, typically with their family's support and blessing but often with their own aspirations and goals for their overseas experience (Martin 2022). These still-malleable cohorts are exposed overseas to new ideas and lifestyles, questioning their own values and practices in universities that often encourage such self-exploration. It is in this context that some Chinese youth encounter the possibilities of social activism for the first time. In Australia, an NGO called the Australia and New Zealand Tongzhi Rainbow Alliance (ANTRA) began in 2013 to support the needs of Chinese-speaking LGBTQIA+ people in the region. With founders including young immigrants from Hong Kong and mainland China, the organization aims to "celebrate and embrace diversity, but most importantly, to become a point-of-contact and support for Mandarin- and Cantonese-speaking LGBTQIA+ community members, particularly migrants, international students and other newly arrived diasporas."[69] At over 3,000 members and growing, the group attracts many "rainbow" people, including a large number from mainland China who are at various stages of study and work. Although their activities largely focus on the social and health needs of ethnic Chinese people living in Australia, the group's diverse members include young mainland Chinese people keen to learn about and support the struggles of *tongzhi* in China.

Another group of recently mobilized activists include participants in the "A4 Movement" that erupted across China in November 2022 out of frustration with government-mandated COVID-19 lockdowns and, in particular, the deaths caused when fire ripped through a locked-down apartment complex in Urumqi, the capital of the Xinjiang Uyghur Autonomous Region. While multiple cities and universities in China saw protests and calls for the CCP to step down, some Chinese youth studying abroad also went to the streets – sometimes masked to protect their identities – to protest and to make demands of the Chinese leadership. Candlelight vigils and other gatherings took place in public spaces and outside Chinese consulates and embassies in many cities, including New York, London, Amsterdam, Paris, Melbourne, Tokyo, and Sydney (Pang 2022). For some of these young people, whether due to observing movements in

---

[69] www.antra.org.au/about-us – Accessed March 27, 2023.

their host countries – like protests around gender discrimination, indigenous rights, and the Russian invasion of Ukraine – or because of events happening within China that rile them and inspire them to action, engaging in street action and organized social movement activity is the possible beginning of a life engaged with any number of social causes.

The nature of sporadic, spontaneous protests and the challenges associated with studying such movements makes it difficult (if not foolish) to draw hard conclusions about the impacts of studying abroad on Chinese youth. Many Chinese students overseas are surely just as apolitical, cynical, career-driven, or risk-averse as their global peers might be. But we also should not underestimate the effect of heightened consciousness about authoritarian practices and the resistances that awareness can engender. As political scientist Rory Truex wrote at the time of the A-4 Movement, "[c]itizens who suddenly recognize the nature of their authoritarian government don't easily forget about it" (Truex 2022).

Chinese young people are increasingly keen to travel abroad, encountering and contemplating the universal values that the party has both embraced and rejected in its own rhetoric. There are numerous variations in motivations and circumstances within the groups that have more recently set out overseas, but the conditions for large-scale emigration and mobility were set in motion in the 1990s by China's increasing wealth, the new travel and study opportunities opened up by globalization, and the privileging of a "Western" education in the global academic hierarchy. These conditions have not fundamentally changed, and early post-pandemic data suggest that interest in studying (and possibly emigrating) overseas continues to remain strong (Wan 2022). According to UNESCO statistics, of the almost 1.1 million Chinese students studying abroad in 2020, about 34 percent studied in the USA, 14 percent in the UK, 12 percent in Australia, and 8 percent in Canada (UNESCO 2021). Political tensions between the USA and China may shift some students away from the USA, in particular, but it is likely that Chinese students will continue to favor this constellation of wealthy democracies, where they will be exposed to the messiness and vibrancy of civil society, regular free elections, and a diversity of social movements and public protests that are typically banned within China itself.

Global civil society's impact on China has not been simply about "doing good" domestically, like supporting orphanages or aged care centers (although those are certainly important). The cosmopolitan ideals articulated by David Held and promoted through transnational networks of activists also resonate with the moral inclinations of many Chinese people, in some cases activating their imaginations of other approaches to international activism. Tom Wang, originally from coal-rich Shanxi province, enjoyed a long career at Greenpeace and other NGOs in China until 2018, when he set off to the Philippines to launch a new, Southeast Asia-based NGO called People of Asia for Climate Solutions. Based in Manila, the group has worked on a range of issues involving Chinese Belt and Road investments, advising Chinese companies on how to make the shift to green technologies and publishing a book on the experiences of local communities impacted directly by BRI-branded projects. Talking with villagers in five Asian countries, the book documents the bad and the good that people have experienced alongside rapid development and massive investments from China, with the authors aiming to speak to both the government of China and other Asian countries: "It is our hope that the stories and perspectives articulated in this book will help compel them to make changes to BRI processes, policies and projects in the interest of the rights and well-being of people and communities, and of environmental, climate, gender and economic justice."[70]

Diaspora activism is a multifaceted phenomenon, with some groups focused on local issues, some groups looking at China's impact in their region, and other groups and individuals engaged in the sorts of transnational activism that actively links movements "at home" in China to social movements outside China, sometimes amplifying the messages of actors within China to the outside world, sometimes projecting messages of solidarity back into China. Regardless of the form diaspora activism takes, however, many such activities are informed by and embedded in the broader goals and aspirations of GCS. They are neither distinctly "Chinese" nor distinctly "foreign," often expressing a shared sense of cosmopolitanism and universally applicable notions of human rights and democratic values that transcend national boundaries.

The direction that this increasingly complex configuration of diaspora activism will take is still uncertain. More than likely, different routes of activism will become even more distinguishable, with some branching out as practices develop and spread to ever larger numbers of people. As an earlier cohort of activists-in-exile come into contact with a newer generation of young students studying abroad, in particular, we might expect certain synergies to emerge whereby the enthusiasm of youth for progressive social change sees people returning to China to start their own organizations, to pick up where those in exile left off, or, perhaps, a time when those in exile feel empowered and secure enough to return home to resume their earlier work. As Zhao (2021) documents and my own contacts in the field confirmed in 2023, some activists who left China to "catch their breath" overseas have already begun to return home to resume their work.

What does diaspora activism mean for the CCP, especially given its repeated criticisms and suspicion of "foreign forces" trying to destabilize China? It may

---

[70] www.brivillage.asia/about/ – Accessed March 28, 2023.

be the first time since Sun Yat-sen and his cohort sought to challenge the Qing court that a government in China has faced such a large – if largely unorganized – group of dissidents and discontents living overseas. To be clear, there seems at present to be no organized opposition keen to dramatically transform – much less "overthrow" – the party-state's ruling system. Also, the Chinese state has at its fingertips technologies of surveillance that did not exist in the late nineteenth and early twentieth centuries. Anyone outside China seeking to even criticize Beijing – much less bring about the downfall of the CCP – can no longer be assumed to be untouchable. The threat and reality of transnational repression is undeniable, thus increasing exponentially the risks experienced by individual activists, their families, and their supporters both inside and outside China. From Uyghurs who are subjected to threats and intimidation abroad (Lemon, Jardine and Hall 2023) to Chinese-Canadians afraid to speak up at public meetings (Al-Jizawi et al. 2022), the long arm of the Chinese state security apparatus is seemingly capable of reaching into almost anyone's homes, work-places, and communities, a phenomenon not unique to China but shared across many authoritarian regimes (Tsourapas 2021). Hong Kong's NSL also asserts extraterritoriality, so that anyone, anywhere in the world who is suspected of the numerous offences listed in the law can be charged by Hong Kong authorities.[71] From university classrooms to media organizations to politicians, the NSL puts everyone worldwide on notice that any statements or actions considered an affront to the security of the Hong Kong government could result in criminal charges.

New technologies of surveillance and repression allow for almost instantan-eous monitoring of diaspora activists (as well as those unconnected by blood or law to China). Although activists who seek to criticize or change practices inside China itself are currently the most obvious targets of Beijing's security apparatus, there is a very short distance between these "traditional" dissidents and groups that highlight problems with China's military and economic activ-ities overseas, for example. Activities that link up activists overseas and those within China are a particular area of concern for state security officials. In early 2023, an organizer of one event to be held outside China was phoned by their closest Chinese consulate, who then transferred the phone call to local police in China so they could discourage the planners from inviting mainland Chinese civil society groups.[72] This chain of events did not stop the event from taking place, but it reduced the participation of Chinese individuals who – still within

---

[71] See Article 38 of "The Law of the People's Republic of China on Safeguarding National Security in the Hong Kong Special Administrative Region."

[72] Details on the event and organizers are withheld here in order to ensure the confidentiality of those involved.

China's borders – were also prevented from traveling abroad to join the event. While repression within China is commonplace for many Chinese civil society actors, it was the first time the group outside China had felt such pressure, and the experience imparted a chilling impression of the power of the Chinese state and the political sensitivities of the issues and people involved.

Conclusion: No Longer a Passive Player

As the third decade of the twenty-first century unfolds, China is no longer simply another country that GCS acts upon. Chinese grassroots NGOs, some GONGOs, and individuals in the Chinese diaspora are increasingly claiming for themselves the universal values promoted by the liberal–democratic version of GCS. Whether it be "going out" with government blessings and financial support or with donations from like-minded compatriots, a variety of groups are taking up the call to care for the environment and their fellow human beings wherever they find them. Young idealists, students, former INGO staffers, and even staid GONGO workers are carrying the banners of their own organizations – and sometimes the Chinese flag – as they look abroad to expand their operations. For the CCP, this is a double-edged sword that comes with obvious risks. Flag-waving and patriotism may motivate many to "go out," but it also risks engendering a backlash from local communities that experience the negative impacts of Chinese investment or have difficulty seeing Chinese NGOs as acting out of purely humanitarian motives.

The universal values that the CCP warns so often against at home, despite their striking similarities to the party's own "socialist core values," are deeply embedded in the works and principles of many INGOs outside China. When Chinese groups and established INGOs come into contact, the basis of their relationship is likely to be these same values, at least rhetorically. The Chinese state thus needs to work extra hard to make sure that when these avowed "socialist" values contradict the realities of life in China, participants in the groups they have sent overseas – in the case of GONGOs, at least – do not reflect back on their own society with a more critical eye. At the same time, keeping tabs on a growing and increasingly disperse, young diaspora requires a vigilance that may be hard for even the PRC state security apparatus to sustain, despite recent advances in technology. Surveillance and the threat – or actuality – of repression further risk engendering a backlash not only from an activist diaspora but also from the societies in which they have settled and to which they are contributing as new residents. Despite the policy developments supporting "going out" and the initial steps some groups have taken to do just that, it is too soon to draw judgments about how Chinese organizations working abroad may converge with or reshape the norms and practices of GCS. Only time will tell whether the Chinese party-state is up to managing the myriad challenges that "going out" inevitably entails and how the established world of INGOs will respond to the entry of Chinese groups.

4 Conclusion and What Lies Ahead

For established GCS actors, the values and ideas that go hand in hand with international NGO work have been developed over decades of experience, experimentation, and reflection on the part of individual staff and organizational leadership. Many of the world's largest INGOs emerged from democratic societies and have been heavily influenced by neoliberal, post-Cold War international and market structures. The cosmopolitan values conveyed through their mission and vision statements reflect their professed commitment to long-standing (if evolving) principles of humanitarianism, democracy, freedom, and human development. They are, in short, key agents of GCS and sites within which cosmopolitan values congeal (Beck 2000; Anheier, Glasius and Kaldor 2005).

With INGOs reentering China in the 1980s and increasing in number after the end of the Cold War, global civil society has had contradictory effects on China. It has offered the Chinese state legal tools, structures, and globally legitimated rhetoric that has been used to depoliticize domestic civil society. At the same time, the introduction of liberal–democratic norms and some specific practices have helped promote awareness of human rights and expanded the inclusivity of political discourse. Although GCS actors may not always live up to their own rhetoric, they have exerted an identifiable demonstration effect on the Chinese state and Chinese civil society, enriching the vocabulary of state and nonstate actors and integrating them into the larger community of global actors concerned with human rights and democracy.

Try as it may, China's leadership is hard-pressed to stem the tide of rights-based ideas and democratic freedoms that hold broad appeal within the country's borders. While much attention has understandably been spent on the impacts of GCS on China, the "going out" of Chinese civil society is arguably the next big chapter of China's global engagement. Given China's size and potential to impact global development, both inbound and outbound GCS engagement deserve continued attention from policymakers, practitioners, and scholars.

Questions Going Forward

Domestically, analyzing INGO registrations, activities, trainings, and ideas will continue to be essential to understanding how authoritarian states like China adapt to the ideological threat posed by GCS. Given the dominance of the Chinese party-state, whether TANs might be able to empower domestic civil society to successfully press for change inside China itself is doubtful. Yet, if there are any spaces in which they can work in the future, what would be the most likely areas of collaboration? And where might we find continuing resistances from the authoritarian state to foreign influence or interference? Matters that can be portrayed and interpreted as "technical" –for example, environmental protection, despite its frequent connection to social and economic inequality – are more likely to comprise areas of cooperation deemed politically acceptable by Beijing and, by extension, local government and civil society actors on the ground in China.

While the impact of GCS on China domestically continues to be relevant for policymakers, academics, and practitioners, the biggest question marks at present are undoubtedly around the "going out" of Chinese civil society organizations. There are indications that BRI as an economic project might already be running out of steam, whether due to a lack of funding in China, concerns about the ability of debtor countries to repay debts, a calculation that the "win–win" Xi imagined is not playing out well for target countries or for China itself, or the pushback from the USA and other countries worried about China's simultaneous military expansion. If these factors intensify and BRI projects diminish in scale or scope, what that means for the internationalization of Chinese civil society is unclear. Will Beijing inject more funding into going out and implement new administrative measures to bolster its soft power push? Or will the state make the calculation that those are not good investments, either, taking political pressure off GONGOs to participate in the "going out" effort?

If the party-state decides to double down on the "going out" of civil society, how target countries will respond is yet another open question. Leah Shipton and Peter Dauvergne (2021) have done researchers a great service in looking at extractive industry investment from BRICS countries and its implications for TANs. In their case study of Ecuador, where Chinese mining enterprises have been backed by a repressive state, "Ecuadorian civil society has been unable to access Chinese courts or government agencies. Nor has Chinese civil society, whether for lack of interest or capacity, widely campaigned in support of Ecuadorian campaigns against Chinese extractive projects" (Shipton and Dauvergne 2021, p. 247). They argue that "China's state-alliance approach, lack of regulatory controls on overseas corporate conduct, and the limited presence of outward-oriented Chinese activism make it a hard-to-hit target for the boomerang strategy" (Shipton and Dauvergne 2021, p. 246). This is perhaps not a surprising finding, but it highlights again how the "boomerang strategy" has, to date, little applicability to China. Without a stronger domestic civil society within China and a critical mass of outward-looking Chinese civil society groups, activists in countries targeted by Chinese enterprises will need to either fight their own battles or turn to more established GCS actors for additional support.

Aside from documenting Chinese nonprofits' overseas activities, future research needs to explore the ideas, values, and practices that they take with them when they leave China. Investigating how their approaches differ from (or are similar to) those promoted by more established INGOs will help both academics and practitioners understand to what extent Chinese efforts complement, enhance, or challenge existing norms and practices in international development. Recalling Schmitz and Mitchell's observations in Section 1, the self-identity of established INGOs is an area that will likely lead to sharp contrasts with Chinese GONGOs, as the former have come to see themselves as "agents of fundamental change committed to accomplishing lofty missions involving not just aid delivery but also the solving of major social, political, economic, and environmental problems" (Schmitz and Mitchell 2022, p. 12). By contrast, the priorities of the Chinese party-state, which will inform official financial and political support for Chinese GONGOs going out, are much more likely to stay clearly within the lines of (superficially) depoliticized charitable activities. China's position on noninterference may be "softening" (Zou and Jones 2020), but Beijing has shown little interest in radically transforming target countries under the banner of universal values (or even "core socialist values").

In practice, though, are Chinese nonprofits strictly following government guidelines or priorities when they decide to work with communities overseas? This is not a simple thing to establish, unless researchers are embedded within GONGOs as they "go out," moving from the home context (China) to the site of overseas operations. Problems of the "architecture" structuring established INGOs outside China – like the lack of beneficiaries on boards and the overriding accountability to donors instead of beneficiaries (Schmitz and Mitchell 2022) – are just as likely (or even more likely) to occur within Chinese GONGOs and grassroots NGOs conducting international programs. Yet transnational solidarity building between Chinese nonprofits and their foreign partners may help bring Chinese groups into closer alignment with larger GCS norms. As Farid and Li (2021) found recently, some INGOs are now assisting and facilitating the "going out" of Chinese groups. How their tutelage will impact the work of Chinese groups moving overseas is still an open question. At this stage, such efforts are unlikely to noticeably shift the work of Chinese government-supported groups working abroad, given resource controls, board controls, and that Beijing's preferred narrative focuses on charitable aid rather than the promotion of any sort of transformative agenda.

Scholarly inquiry into the internationalization of Chinese civil society is still in its infancy. We understand too little about whether the grassroots Chinese NGOs and GONGOs engaging in overseas ventures are similar in their motivations, impacts, and the lessons they learn when working overseas. Indeed, it is not clear yet how the experiences of GONGOs and grassroots NGOs may differ as they internationalize their work. As one former GONGO-turned INGO worker recounted in an interview, at least a few prominent Chinese GONGOs have largely embraced the role of "flag-wavers" when going out to other countries, promoting Chinese state narratives about Chinese contributions to host-country prosperity but doing little to connect with, much less empower local populations. Whether that is broadly true is an open question. It might also be that the experiences of GONGOs and grassroots groups differ substantially, whereby grassroots groups, more influenced by the norms of GCS due to their greater exposure to and (sometimes) collaboration with INGOs in China, are more likely to work in tune with mainstream GCS principles. Relatedly, given the more direct ideological and institutional constraints on GONGOs, it may be that overseas expansion will serve to reinforce rather than bridge the normative and practical divergences between Chinese GONGOs and grassroots NGOs in China and in their work abroad. Most broadly, the collective impact on other countries – and on GCS norms themselves – of GONGOs' and grassroots NGOs' going out is yet to be seen, as the scale of operations of both sorts of groups is still quite small. Assuming that any future expansion of government support benefits GONGOs most directly, where does that leave grassroots NGOs' efforts to engage *as* members of a GCS underpinned by normative commitments to universal values?

Dozens of other questions remain about the perceived drivers and experiences of groups that go abroad. Included among these must be the following questions: How have Chinese nonprofits been received in host countries? How have Chinese nonprofits interacted with Chinese enterprises overseas? What roles have INGOs played in facilitating Chinese NGOs' going out? What kinds of encounters with local civil society and INGOs in other countries have Chinese NGOs experienced? How have those encounters affected their work and development? What kinds of values and ideas form the basis for Chinese nonprofits overseas activities? What challenges have Chinese nonprofits faced in going out, and have they changed over time? What kinds of material and nonmaterial resources have been mobilized – from government, businesses, and the general public – to support Chinese nonprofits going out? How are China's newly emergent philanthropic foundations – many of which are driven by individual entrepreneurs and the companies they have founded – approaching the "going out" drive?

We also need to study the ways in which GCS's norms and values inform or contrast with the principles underpinning both GONGOs and grassroots NGOs' overseas activities. As seen from Chinese groups and their overseas partners or local societies, do grassroots NGOs behave differently from GONGOs when they implement projects? What can any such differences in turn tell us about GCS? While existing literature notes a range of factors at play that impact GCS effectiveness, there is little research on how GCS actors evolve within specific sociohistorical contexts (Anderson and Zaloznaya 2018).

Many other empirical questions remain and will be more consequential if Chinese NGOs' overseas activities grow as expected. For example, is there a concentration of Chinese activities in particular regions of the world and, if so, what explains that? What are the main types of work and aid Chinese nonprofits are delivering or pursuing? What has driven the priorities of different sorts of actors – political pressures from Beijing, economic considerations, or more idealistic goals? Are they pursuing long-term relationships or one-off projects? As Lecy has shown, in the USA "80 per cent of the funds that pass through the international subsector are controlled by three percent of the organizations, with the top one per cent garnering 60 per cent of total funds" (Lecy 2012, p. 2, cited in Elizabeth A. Bloodgood and Hans Peter Schmitz 2013, p. 70). If China's "going out" follows a similar trajectory, we might expect that the majority of Chinese funds will be controlled by a relatively small set of GONGOs. Given the tight controls over civil society registration in China and the perceived political significance of Chinese overseas aid projects, state controls may result in an even higher concentration of funds in the hands of a few favored entities.

Investigating the links and interactions between the Chinese state, for-profit enterprises, and nonprofit organizations would place the work of Chinese NGOs into a multidimensional context that speaks both to academic interests and to the concerns of practitioners. Understanding how Chinese groups' approaches differ (or are similar to) the dominant norms and practices promoted by more established INGOs will help both academics and practitioners understand to what extent Chinese efforts complement, enhance, or challenge existing norms and practices in international development. Most broadly, the careful study of Chinese nonprofits' global presence and impact could greatly advance the theoretical conceptualization of GCS in a post-unipolar international system.

Tentatively, it seems that the case of China should prompt us to set aside some of the assumptions about the future of GCS that dominated the earliest, idealistic articulations of the concept. Just as the end of the Cold War did not usher in the "end of history" (Fukuyama 1989), sweeping the world into an unquestioned era of liberal democracy (and capitalism), the proliferation of INGOs over the past few decades has not precluded the rise of populism, authoritarian regimes, and democratic backsliding in Asia and other parts of the world. China's entry into the field of GCS – even if it is still predominantly on the periphery – creates a new opportunity to test the universal appeal of Held's cosmopolitanism and also the strength or tenuousness of authoritarian claims over much of the world's population.

Deng Xiaoping's reform agenda opened China not only to new economic models and trade opportunities. It also meant – at least for a few decades – that foreign NGOs were welcomed to bring in the myriad of new ideas and new ways of doing things that Zhao Liqing so adeptly acknowledged in 2006. Four decades after Deng's about-face on Chinese economic development, and as Xi Jinping's unprecedented third term gets underway, there are now many signs that the window may be almost fully shut for GCS activities inside China. Restrictions abound, and the political rhetoric about nefarious foreign forces threatening China is arguably at a new high. Conversely, the door allowing the "going out" of Chinese civil society – including diverse forms of diaspora activism – seems to have just been opened. If practice follows policy, then we should expect to see China engaging with GCS *outside* of China more fully in the coming years. What form that engagement will take, how Chinese practices will be exported to other places, how pre-existing GCS actors meet their Chinese counterparts in the field, and the impacts on communities outside China's borders are yet to be seen.

References

United Nations Office n Geneva (UNOG) *5th Meeting, 73rd Session, Committee on Economic, Social and Cultural Rights (CESCR)* (2023). https://media.un.org/en/asset/k10/k10ledzwso (Accessed: April 25, 2023).

Albert, E. (2017) *Backgrounder: China in Africa.* New York: Council on Foreign Relations. www.cfr.org/backgrounder/china-africa (Accessed: August 4, 2023).

Al-Jizawi, N. et al. (2022) *Psychological and Emotional War: Digital Transnational Repression in Canada,* 151. Toronto: University of Toronto. https://tspace.library.utoronto.ca/bitstream/1807/120575/1/Report%23151–dtr_022822_lowres.pdf.

Amnesty International. (2021) "Amnesty International to Close Its Hong Kong Offices," October 25. www.amnesty.org/en/latest/news/2021/10/amnesty-international-to-close-its-hong-kong-offices/ (Accessed: April 6, 2023).

Anderson, E., and Zaloznaya, M. (2018) "Global Civil Society and the Test of Kyoto: A Theoretical Extension," *International Journal of Comparative Sociology,* 59(3), pp. 179–211. https://doi.org/10.1177/0020715218776411.

Anderson, K., and Rieff, D. (2005) *"Global Civil Society": A Sceptical View.* SSRN Scholarly Paper ID 899771. Rochester, NY: Social Science Research Network. http://papers.ssrn.com/abstract=899771 (Accessed: February 10, 2014).

Anheier, H. K., Glasius, M., and Kaldor, M. (2001) "Introducing Global Civil Society," in H. K. Anheier, M. Glasius, and M. Kaldor (eds.) *Global Civil Society 2001,* pp. 3–22. www.lse.ac.uk/internationalDevelopment/research/CSHS/civilSociety/yearBook/contentsPages/2001.aspx (Accessed: February 21, 2014).

Anheier, H. K., Glasius, M., and Kaldor, M. (2005) "Country Participation in INGOs," in H. K. Anheier, M. Glasius, and M. Kaldor (eds.) *Global Civil Society 2004/05.* London: Sage, pp. 304–309.

Beck, U. (2000) "The Cosmopolitan Perspective: Sociology of the Second Age of Modernity," *British Journal of Sociology,* 51(1), pp. 79–105. https://doi.org/10.1080/000713100358444.

Bewicke, A. E. (2016) "From 'Eating the Rice' to Sipping Starbucks: China's Emerging Relationship with Universal Criminal Justice Norms and the Role of External Actors," in T. C. Chen, and D. Chen (eds.) *International Engagement in China's Human Rights.*(China policy series, 40) New York: Routledge, pp. 46–61.

Bloodgood, E. A., and Schmitz, H. P. (2013) "The INGO Research Agenda," in B. Reinalda (ed.) *Routledge Handbook of International Organization.*

Abingdon: Routledge, pp. 67–79. https://doi.org/10.4324/9780203405 345.ch5.

Bob, C. (2009) "Introduction: Fighting for New Rights," in C. Bob (ed.) *The International Struggle for New Human Rights*. Philadelphia: University of Pennsylvania Press, pp. 1–13. https://doi.org/10.9783/9780812201345.

Brenner, D. (2012). "Are Chinese NGOs 'Going out'? The Role of Chinese NGOs and GONGOs in Sino-African Relations." *Journal of Public and International Affairs*, 22(1), pp. 131–152.

Burton-Bradley, R. (2022) *Has China's Push to Ban 'Effeminate' and 'Sissy' Men Claimed Its First Victim? The Tragic Case of Zhou Peng, The South China Morning Post*. www.scmp.com/news/people-culture/gender-diversity/ article/3162053/has-chinas-push-ban-effeminate-and-sissy-men (Accessed: April 25, 2023).

Carpenter, C. (2009) "Orphaned Again? Children Born of Wartime Rape as a Non-Issue for the Human Rights Movement," in C. Bob (ed.) *The International Struggle for New Human Rights*. Philadelphia: University of Pennsylvania Press, pp. 14–29. https://doi.org/10.9783/9780812201345.

Carpenter, C., Duygulu S., Montgomery, A. H., & Rapp A. (2014) "Explaining the Advocacy Agenda: Insights from the Human Security Network," *International Organization*, 68(2), pp. 449–470. https://doi.org/10.1017/ S0020818313000453.

Chan, K. (2015) "Occupying Hong Kong: How Deliberation, Referendum, and Civil Disobedience Played Out in the Umbrella Movement," *International Journal on Human Rights*, 12(21), pp. 1–7.

Chen, J. (2012) *Transnational Civil Society in China: Intrusion and Impact*. Northampton: Edward Elgar.

China Development Brief. (2023) *CDB Projects Map, China Development Brief*. https://chinadevelopmentbrief.org/projects-map-en/ (Accessed: April 29, 2023).

China Times. "Minzhengbu: Jiaqiang Jingwai NGO Lai Guonei Huodong Dengji Guanli" (Ministry of Civil Affairs: Strengthen the Registration and Management of Activities by INGOs in China)." *China Times*, September 20, 2013. http://www.chinanews.com/gn/2012/09-20/4198753.shtml.

ChinaFile. (2013) *Document 9: A ChinaFile Translation –How Much Is a Hardline Party Directive Shaping China's Current Political Climate?*, *ChinaFile*. www.chinafile.com/document-9-chinafile-translation (Accessed: September 1, 2020).

Chinese International Education Foundation. (2023) *About CIEF*. www.cief .org.cn/jj (Accessed: May 5, 2023).

Cooley, A., and Ron, J. (2010) "The Political Economy of Transnational Action among International NGOs," in A. Prakash and M. K. Gugerty (eds.) *Advocacy Organizations and Collective Action*. Cambridge: Cambridge University Press, pp. 205–228. https://doi.org/10.1017/CBO9780511762635.012.

Dai, F. (2020) "Feizhengfuzuzhi zai meiguo dui wai zhanlue zhong de zuoyong qianxi," *Zhongguo Renmin Daxue Xuebao*, 4, pp. 113–124.

Devlin, K., and Ni, V. (2017) *Chinese Gay Video Ban Sparks Online Backlash*, BBC News. www.bbc.com/news/blogs-trending-40610679 (Accessed: April 25, 2023).

Drainville, André C. (2005) "Beyond Altermondialisme: Anti-Capitalist Dialectic of Presence." *Review of International Political Economy* 12(5), pp. 884–908. https://doi.org/10.1080/09692290500339875.

Farid, M., and Li, H. (2021) "International NGOs as Intermediaries in China's 'going out' Strategy," *International Affairs*, 97(6), pp. 1945–1962. https://doi.org/10.1093/ia/iiab183.

Farid, M., and Song, C. (2020) "Public Trust as a Driver of State-Grassroots NGO Collaboration in China," *Journal of Chinese Political Science*, 25(4), pp. 591–613. https://doi.org/10.1007/s11366-020-09691-7.

Fonte, J. (2004) "Democracy's Trojan Horse," *National Interest*, (76), pp. 117–127.

Ford Foundation. (2005) *Annual Report*. www.fordfoundation.org/wp-content/uploads/2015/03/ar2005.pdf.

Franceschini, I., and Negro, G. (2014) "The "Jasmine Revolution" in China: The limits of the Cyber-Utopia," *Postcolonial Studies*, 17(1), pp. 23–35. https://doi.org/10.1080/13688790.2014.912190.

Fu, D. (2017) "Disguised Collective Action in China," *Comparative Political Studies*, 50(4), pp. 499–527. https://doi.org/10.1177/0010414015626437.

Fukuyama, F. (1989) "The End of History?," *The National Interest*, (16), pp. 3–18.

Gao, X. (2010) "From the Heyang Model to the Shaanxi Model: Action Research on Women's Participation in Village Governance," *The China Quarterly*, 204, pp. 870–898. https://doi.org/10.1017/S0305741010001001.

Gow, M. (2017) "The Core Socialist Values of the Chinese Dream: Towards a Chinese Integral State," *Critical Asian Studies*, 49(1), pp. 92–116. https://doi.org/10.1080/14672715.2016.1263803.

Hsu, J. Y., Hildebrandt, T., & Hasmath, R. (2016). "Going out'or staying in? The expansion of Chinese NGOs in Africa." *Development Policy Review*, 34(3), pp. 423–439.

Held, D. (2003) "Cosmopolitanism: Taming Globalization," in D. Held, and A. G. McGrew (eds.) *The Global Transformations Reader: An Introduction to the Globalization Debate*. 2nd ed. Cambridge: Polity Press, pp. 514–529. D Blackwell Pub.

Hildebrandt, T. (2013) *Social Organizations and the Authoritarian State in China*. New York: Cambridge University Press.

Hsiung, P.-C., Jaschok, M., and Milwertz, C. N. (eds.) (2001) *Chinese Women Organizing: Cadres, Feminists, Muslims, Queers*. Oxford: Berg.

Huang, Q. (2023) "Anti-Feminism: Four Strategies for the Demonisation and Depoliticisation of Feminism on Chinese Social Media," *Feminist Media Studies*, 23(7), pp. 3583–3598. https://doi.org/10.1080/14680777.2022 .2129412.

Jalloh, A.-B., and Wan, F. (2019) "Resistance Growing to Chinese Presence in Zambia," *Deutsche Welle*, April 9. www.dw.com/en/resistance-growing-to-chinese-presence-in-zambia/a-47275927 (Accessed: August 4, 2023).

Jordan, L. (2011) "Global Civil Society," in M. Edwards (ed.) *The Oxford Handbook of Civil Society*. 1st ed. Oxford: Oxford University Press, pp. 93–106. https://doi.org/10.1093/oxfordhb/9780195398571.013.0008.

Junker, A. (2019) *Becoming Activists in Global China: Social Movements in the Chinese Diaspora*. Cambridge: Cambridge University Press.

Kaldor, M. (2003) *Global Civil Society: An Answer to War*. Cambridge: Polity Press.

Kaldor, M., Anheier, H. K., and Glasius, M. (2005) "Introduction," in M. Glasius, M. Kaldor, and H. K. Anheier (eds.) *Global Civil Society 2004/05*. London: Sage, pp. 1–22.

Kastner, S., L., Pearson, M. M., and Rector, C. (2018). *China's Strategic Multilateralism: Investing in Global Governance*. Cambridge: Cambridge University Press.

Keane, John. (2001). "Global Civil Society?" In *Global Civil Society 2001*, edited by Helmut K. Anheier, Marlies Glasius, and Mary Kaldor. Oxford: Oxford University Press, pp. 23–47.

Keck, M. E., and Sikkink, K. (1998) *Activists Beyond Borders: Advocacy Networks in International Politics*. Ithaca: Cornell University Press.

Keech-Marx, S. (2008) "Airing Dirty Laundry in Public: Anti-domestic Violence Activism in Beijing," in J. Unger (ed.) *Associations and the Chinese State: Contested Spaces*. M.E. Sharpe. New York: Routledge, pp. 175–199.

Kellogg, T. E. (2012) "Western Funding for Rule of Law Initiatives in China," *China Perspectives*, 2012(3), pp. 53–59.

Kennedy, S. ed., (2018). *Global governance and China: The Dragon's learning curve*. New York: Routledge.

Kent, A. (2002) "China's International Socialization: The Role of International Organizations," *Global Governance*, 8(3), pp. 343–364.

Korten, D. C., Perlas, N., and Shiva, V. (2002) "Global Civil Society: The Path Ahead" www.pcdf.org/civilsociety/path.htm (Accessed: April 13, 2007).

Lai, W., and Spires, A. J. (2021) "Marketization and Its Discontents: Unveiling the Impacts of Foundation-Led Venture Philanthropy on Grassroots NGOs in China," *The China Quarterly*, 245, pp. 72–93. https://doi.org/10.1017/S0305 741020000193.

Lecy, J. D. (2012) *Competition in Growing NGO Sectors*. Syracuse: Moynihan Institute of Global Affairs.

Lecy, J. D., Mitchell, G. E., and Peter Schmitz, H. (2010) "Advocacy Organizations, Networks, and the Firm Analogy," in A. Prakash, and M. K. Gugerty (eds.) *Advocacy Organizations and Collective Action*. Cambridge: Cambridge University Press, pp. 229–251. https://doi.org/10.1017/CBO97 80511762635.013.

Leggett, A. (2017) "Online Civic Engagement and the Anti-domestic Violence Movement in China: Shifting Norms and Influencing Law," *Voluntas: International Journal of Voluntary and Nonprofit Organizations*, 28, pp. 2251–2277. https://doi.org/10.1007/s11266-016-9680-9.

Lemon, E., Jardine, B., and Hall, N. (2023) "Globalizing Minority Persecution: China's Transnational Repression of the Uyghurs," *Globalizations*, 20(4), pp. 564–580. https://doi.org/10.1080/14747731.2022.2135944.

Leslie, A. N. (2016) "Zambia and China: Workers' Protest, Civil Society and the Role of Opposition Politics in Elevating State Engagement," *African Studies Quarterly*, 16(3–4), pp. 89–106.

Lewis, J. I. (2020) "China's Low-Carbon Energy Strategy," in A. Esarey, M. A. Haddad, J. I. Lewis, and S. Harrell (eds.) *Greening East Asia*. University of Washington Press, pp. 47–61. https://doi.org/10.2307/j.ctv19rs1b2.

Li, T. (2004) "Weishenme bu shuo," in Z. Li (ed.) *Dagong shidai No. 1: Zhiye zhi tong*. Beijing: Huaxia Chubanshe (Dagong Times, 1), pp. 3–5.

Li, X., and Dong, Q. (2018) "Chinese NGOs Are 'Going Out': History, Scale, Characteristics, Outcomes, And Barriers." *Nonprofit Policy Forum*, 9(1), pp. 1–9.

Long, Y. (2018) "The Contradictory Impact of Transnational AIDS Institutions on State Repression in China, 1989–2013," *American Journal of Sociology*, 124(2), pp. 309–366. https://doi.org/10.1086/698466.

Lowenkron, B. F. (2006) "The Essential Role of Non-Governmental Organizations in the Development of Democracy" https://2001-2009.state.gov/g/drl/rls/rm/2006/68658.htm (Accessed: January 9, 2023).

Lu, J., and Peng, B. (2018) "Chinese NGOs 'Going Out': Handbook for Working in Nepal. Beijing: China Foundation for Poverty Alleviation." (in Chinese).

Lu, J. (2021) "The Yirenping Experience: Looking Back and Pushing Forward," *Made in China*, 15 July. https://madeinchinajournal.com/2021/07/15/the-yir enping-experience-looking-back-and-pushing-forward/ (Accessed: March 20, 2023).

Lugar, R. G. (2006) *The Backlash Against Democracy Assistance: A Report Prepared by the National Endowment for Democracy for Senator Richard G. Lugar, Chairman, Committee on Foreign Relations, United States Senate.* Washington, DC: National Endowment for Democracy.

Martin, F. (2022) *Dreams of Flight: The Lives of Chinese Women Students in the West.* Durham: Duke University Press.

Morton, K. (2005) "The Emergence of NGOs in China and Their Transnational Linkages: Implications for Domestic Reform," *Australian Journal of International Affairs*, 59(4), pp. 519–532. https://doi.org/10.1080/103577 10500367315.

Noakes, S. (2018) *The Advocacy Trap: Transnational Activism and State Power in China.* Manchester: Manchester University Press (Alternative Sinology).

Noakes, S. and Teets, J. C. (2020) "Learning Under Authoritarianism: Strategic Adaptations within International Foundations and NGOs in China," *Voluntas: International Journal of Voluntary and Nonprofit Organizations*, 31(5), pp. 1093–1113. https://doi.org/10.1007/s11266-017-9939-9.

Pang, J. (2022) "China's lockdown protests spread to campuses and cities abroad," *Reuters*, 29 November. www.reuters.com/world/china/chinas-pro tests-over-lockdowns-spread-campuses-communities-abroad-2022-11-28/ (Accessed: March 27, 2023).

Peck, J., and Tickell, A. (2002) "Neoliberalizing Space," *Antipode*, 34(3), pp. 380–404. https://doi.org/10.1111/1467-8330.00247.

Penghao Theater (2013) "The 4th Beijing Nanluoguxiang Performing Arts Festival" Beijing: Penghao Theater.

Ramia, G. (2003) "Global Social Policy, INGOs and Strategic Management An Emerging Research Agenda," *Global Social Policy*, 3(1), pp. 79–101. https://doi.org/10.1177/1468018103003001540.

Redvers, L. (2011) "The Rise and Rise of China in Zambia," *Mail and Guardian*. Online, September 9. https://mg.co.za/article/2011-09-09-the-rise-and-of-china-in-zambia/ (Accessed: August 4, 2023).

Repnikova, M. (2022) *Chinese Soft Power.* 1st ed. Cambridge: Cambridge University Press. https://doi.org/10.1017/9781108874700.

Richburg, K. B. (2010) "China's Crackdown on Nonprofit Groups Prompts New Fears Among Activists," *The Washington Post*, May 11. www.washing

tonpost.com/wp-dyn/content/article/2010/05/10/AR2010051004801_pf.html.

Sautman, B., and Yan, H. (2014) "Bashing 'the Chinese': Contextualizing Zambia's Collum Coal Mine shooting," *Journal of Contemporary China*, 23(90), pp. 1073–1092. https://doi.org/10.1080/10670564.2014.898897.

Schmitz, H. P., and Mitchell, G. E. (2022) "Understanding the Limits of Transnational NGO Power: Forms, Norms, and the Architecture," *International Studies Review*, 24(3), p. viac042. https://doi.org/10.1093/isr/viac042.

Sénit, C., and Biermann, F. (2021) "In Whose Name Are You Speaking? The Marginalization of the Poor in Global Civil Society," *Global Policy*, 12(5), pp. 581–591. https://doi.org/10.1111/1758-5899.12997.

Setiawan, K. M. P., and Spires, A. J. (2021) "Global Concepts, Local Meanings: How Civil Society Interprets and Uses Human Rights in Asia," *Asian Studies Review*, 45(1), pp. 1–12. https://doi.org/10.1080/10357823.2020.1849028.

Shambaugh, D. (2015) "China's Soft-Power Push: The Search for Respect," *Foreign Affairs*, 94(4), pp. 99–107.

Shieh, S., Lowell C., Zhong H., and Jinfei Y. (2021) *Understanding and Mitigating Social Risks to Sustainable Development in China's BRI: Evidence from Nepal and Zambia*. London: Overseas Development Institute. www.econstor.eu/bitstream/10419/251126/1/176461657X.pdf.

Shipton, L., and Dauvergne, P. (2021) "The Politics of Transnational Advocacy Against Chinese, Indian, and Brazilian Extractive Projects in the Global South," *The Journal of Environment & Development*, 30(3), pp. 240–264. https://doi.org/10.1177/10704965211019083.

Sidel, M. (2019) "Managing the Foreign: The Drive to Securitize Foreign Nonprofit and Foundation Management in China," *Voluntas: International Journal of Voluntary and Nonprofit Organizations*, 30(4), pp. 664–677. https://doi.org/10.1007/s11266-018-9988-8.

Spires, A. J. (2011a) "Contingent Symbiosis and Civil Society in an Authoritarian State: Understanding the Survival of China's Grassroots NGOs," *American Journal of Sociology*, 117(1), pp. 1–45. https://doi.org/10.1086/660741.

Spires, A. J. (2011b) "Organizational Homophily in International Grantmaking: US-Based Foundations and their Grantees in China," *Journal of Civil Society*, 7(3), pp. 305–331. https://doi.org/10.1080/17448689.2011.605005.

Spires, A. J. (2012) "Lessons from Abroad: Foreign Influences on China's Emerging Civil Society," *China Journal*, 68), pp. 125–146.

Spires, A. J. (2020) "Regulation as Political Control: China's First Charity Law and Its Implications for Civil Society," *Nonprofit and Voluntary Sector Quarterly*, 49(3), pp. 571–588. https://doi.org/10.1177/0899764019883939.

Spires, A. J. (2022) "Built on Shifting Sands: INGOs and their Survival in China," in A. J. Spires and A. Ogawa (eds.) *Authoritarianism and Civil Society in Asia*. New York: Routledge, pp. 218–234.

Spires, A. J., Tao, Lin, and Chan, K. (2014) "Societal Support for China's Grass-Roots NGOs: Evidence from Yunnan, Guangdong and Beijing," *The China Journal*, 71, pp. 65–90. https://doi.org/10.1086/674554.

Theo, R., and Leung, M. W. H. (2018) "China's Confucius Institute in Indonesia: Mobility, Frictions and Local Surprises," *Sustainability*, 10(2), p. 530. https://doi.org/10.3390/su10020530.

Tian, F., and Chuang, J. (2022) "Depoliticizing China's Grassroots NGOs: State and Civil Society as an Institutional Field of Power," *The China Quarterly*, 250, pp. 509–530. https://doi.org/10.1017/S0305741022000157.

Truex, R. (2022) "China's Blank-Paper Protests Are Only a Beginning," *The Atlantic*, December 2. www.theatlantic.com/ideas/archive/2022/12/chinas-next-revolution-doesnt-have-to-be-immediate/672327/ (Accessed: March 27, 2023).

Tsourapas, G. (2021) "Global Autocracies: Strategies of Transnational Repression, Legitimation, and Co-optation in World Politics," *International Studies Review*, 23(3), pp. 616–644. https://doi.org/10.1093/isr/viaa061.

Tvedt, T. (1998) *Angels of Mercy or Development Diplomats?: NGOs & Foreign Aid*. Trenton, NJ: Africa World Press.

UNESCO, I. for S. (2021) *Global Flow of Tertiary-Level Students*. UNESCO Institute for Statistics. http://uis.unesco.org/en/uis-student-flow#slideout menu (Accessed: March 24, 2023).

United Nations, O. of the H.C. for H.R. (2022) *OHCHR Assessment of human rights concerns in the Xinjiang Uyghur Autonomous Region, People's Republic of China*. Geneva: United Nations. www.ohchr.org/sites/default/files/documents/countries/2022-08-31/22-08-31-final-assesment.pdf.

Vlassis, A. (2016). "Soft Power, Global Governance of Cultural Industries and Rising Powers: The Case of China." *International Journal of Cultural Policy*, 22 (4), pp. 481–496.

Wan, X. (2022) "Will Chinese International Student Numbers Rebound in the US?," *University World News*, October 21. www.universityworldnews.com/post.php?story=20221019111638139 (Accessed: March 24, 2023).

Wang, H. (2007) "'Linking Up with the International Track' What's in a Slogan?," *The China Quarterly*. 2007/03/16 edn., 189, pp. 1–23. https://doi.org/10.1017/S0305741006000774.

Wang, S. (2013) "'Gongmin Shehui': Xin Ziyou Zhuyi Bianzao de Cucao Shenhua." Renmin Luntan Zhenglun Shuangzhoukan, no. 412. http://theory

.people.com.cn/n/2013/0808/c40531-22488604-3.html (Accessed: December 30, 2022).

Wang, Y. R. (2016) "The Changed and Unchanged in Chinese Religious Freedom Discourse and its Responses to International Engagement of Protestant Advocacy," in T. C. Chen and D. Chen (eds.) *International Engagement in China's Human Rights*. (China policy series, 40) New York: Routledge, pp. 113–133.

Wilson, J. L. (2009) "Coloured Revolutions: The View from Moscow and Beijing," *Journal of Communist Studies and Transition Politics*, 25(2–3), pp. 369–395. https://doi.org/10.1080/13523270902861061.

Wu, F. (2011) "Strategic State Engagement in Transnational Activism: AIDS Prevention in China," *Journal of Contemporary China*, 20(71), pp. 621–637. https://doi.org/10.1080/10670564.2011.587162.

Xi, J. (2015) "Chinese President Xi Jinping Addresses the American Public" Seattle, WA, September 22. www.ncuscr.org/event/chinese-president-xi-jinping-addresses-american-public/ (Accessed: April 6, 2023).

Xi, J. (2022) "Xi Jinping zai zhongguo gongchandang diershici quanguo daibiao dahui shang de baogao," Xinhuanet, October 25. www.news.cn/politics/cpc20/2022-10/25/c_1129079429.htm (Accessed: April 30, 2023).

Xu, D. (2020) "Cong Meiguo xin 'zhengzhizhan' kan guoji feizhengfuzuzhi dailai de zhengzhi fengxian," *Changjiang Luntan*, 1, pp. 46–51.

Xu, X. (2022) "Tuidong gongyi cishan lingyu de 'xingbie zhuliuhua,' zenme zuo?," 9 December. https://mp.weixin.qq.com/s/KQUoS-1PhuePMs EssryqDA (Accessed: April 11, 2023).

Yang, G. (2003) "The Internet and the Rise of a Transnational Chinese Cultural Sphere," *Media, Culture & Society*, 25(4), pp. 469–490. https://doi.org/10.1177/01634437030254003.

Yang, L. (2022) "Controversial Confucius Institutes Returning to U.S. Schools Under New Name," *VOA*, June 27. www.voanews.com/a/controversial-confucius-institutes-returning-to-u-s-schools-under-new-name/6635906.html (Accessed: May 5, 2023).

Yuen, S. (2015) "Friend or Foe? The Diminishing Space of China's Civil Society," *China Perspectives*, 3, pp. 51–56.

Zhang, N. (2001) "Searching for 'Authentic' NGOs: The NGO Discourse and Women's Organizations in China," in P.-C. Hsiung, M. Jaschok, and C. Milwert (eds.) *Chinese Women Organizing: Cadres, Feminists, Muslims, Queers*. Oxford: Berg, pp. 159–179.

Zhang, Y., and Buzan, B. (2020) "China and the Global Reach of Human Rights," *The China Quarterly*, 241, pp. 169–190. https://doi.org/10.1017/S0305741019000833.

Zhao, J., Du, J., and Wen, Y. (eds.) (2008) *Tigao cunweihui nvganbu lingdao nengli*. 1st edn. Xi'an: Xibei Daxue Chubanshe.

Zhao, L. (2006) "Ruhe kandai zai zhongguo de waiguo de feizhengfu zuzhi (How to View Foreign NGOs in China)," *Study Times*. www.studytimes.com .cn/txt/2006-08/21/content_7094045.htm.

Zhao, M. (2021) "Solidarity Stalled: When Chinese Activists Meet Social Movements in Democracies," *Critical Sociology*, 47(2), pp. 281–297. https://doi.org/10.1177/0896920520940007.

Zhao, R., Wu, Z., and Tao, C. (2016) "Understanding Service Contracting and Its Impact on NGO Development in China," *Voluntas: International Journal of Voluntary and Nonprofit Organizations*, 27(5), pp. 2229–2251. https://doi .org/10.1007/s11266-016-9714-3.

Zhou, B. (2011) "Zou zhongguo tese shehui guanli chuangxin zhi lu," *Qiushi*, 10. www.qstheory.cn/zxdk/2011/2011010/201105/t20110513_80501.htm (Accessed: May 1, 2016).

Zhou, Y., and Luk, S. (2016) "Establishing Confucius Institutes: A Tool for Promoting China's Soft Power?," *Journal of Contemporary China*, 25(100), pp. 628–642. https://doi.org/10.1080/10670564.2015.1132961.

Zou, Y., and Jones, L. (2020) "China's Response to Threats to Its Overseas Economic Interests: Softening Non-Interference and Cultivating Hegemony," *Journal of Contemporary China*, 29(121), pp. 92–108. https:// doi.org/10.1080/10670564.2019.1621532.

Acknowledgments

This Element draws in part on work I have published since 2011. Section 1 expands on my contribution to an article co-authored with Ken Setiawan in *Asian Studies Review* (Setiawan and Spires 2021). Sections 1 and 2 draw on a perspective on the GCS literature I first introduced in a chapter of *Authoritarianism and Civil Society in Asia* (Spires 2022) which I co-edited with Akihiro Ogawa. Section 2 also draws on articles I published in *The China Journal* (Spires 2012), the *Nonprofit and Voluntary Sector Quarterly* (Spires 2020), and *The Journal of Civil Society* (Spires 2011b). I am grateful to my collaborators in many fields who helped me hone the arguments and expanded both my knowledge and perspective on what my research in China and elsewhere has revealed over the years. This Element has benefited tremendously from a series of conversations, questions, and comments from colleagues, including Fengshi Wu, Weijun Lai, Tim Hildebrandt, Kin-man Chan, Jessica Teets, Rachel Stern, and many students in my classrooms at the Chinese University of Hong Kong and the University of Melbourne. Any mistakes or omissions are entirely my responsibility. The research underpinning this Element was supported in part by a General Research Fund grant from the Hong Kong Research Grants Council (RGC Ref No. 450013, "Global Civil Society and China: Making Sense of International Nongovernmental Organizations in an Authoritarian State"). I am thankful to Ching Kwan Lee for the invitation to contribute to the Elements series, and for giving me the opportunity to weave together my thoughts and research on these topics. I am grateful to the anonymous reviewers at Cambridge University Press and especially to the many actors within Chinese civil society and global civil society who have shared their perspectives, struggles, and hopes with me. I hope I have done justice to their stories in my depictions of the world they inhabit. Finally, I thank my partner, Reiser Yu, and our child, Riley, for their patience and understanding as I worked to complete this project.

Cambridge Elements ⁼

Global China

Ching Kwan Lee
University of California-Los Angeles

Ching Kwan Lee is professor of sociology at the University of California-Los Angeles. Her scholarly interests include political sociology, popular protests, labor, development, political economy, comparative ethnography, China, Hong Kong, East Asia and the Global South. She is the author of three multiple award-winning monographs on contemporary China: Gender and the South China Miracle: Two Worlds of Factory Women (1998), Against the Law: Labor Protests in China's Rustbelt and Sunbelt (2007), and The Specter of Global China: Politics, Labor and Foreign Investment in Africa (2017). Her co-edited volumes include Take Back Our Future: an Eventful Sociology of Hong Kong's Umbrella Movement (2019) and The Social Question in the 21st Century: A Global View (2019).

About the Series

The Cambridge Elements series Global China showcases thematic, region- or country-specific studies on China's multifaceted global engagements and impacts. Each title, written by a leading scholar of the subject matter at hand, combines a succinct, comprehensive and up-to-date overview of the debates in the scholarly literature with original analysis and a clear argument. Featuring cutting edge scholarship on arguably one of the most important and controversial developments in the 21st century, the Global China Elements series will advance a new direction of China scholarship that expands China Studies beyond China's territorial boundaries.

Cambridge Elements ≡

Global China

Milton Keynes UK
Ingram Content Group UK Ltd.
UKHW020813080424
440801UK00015B/839

9 781009 184168